Library of
Davidson College

HAROLD LASKI

Harold Laski

by

GRANVILLE EASTWOOD

MOWBRAYS
LONDON & OXFORD

© 1977 A. R. Mowbray & Co. Ltd.

First published by A. R. Mowbray & Co. Ltd.
Saint Thomas House, Becket St., Oxford, OX1 1SJ

ISBN 0 264 66466 3

Text set in 11/12 pt. Intertype Baskerville, printed by
Western Printing Services Ltd, Bristol.

CONTENTS

Foreword   vii

Author's Note   x

CHAPTER 1   Early Days in England and North America   1

CHAPTER 2   Teacher and Friend   20

CHAPTER 3   People and Politics   44

CHAPTER 4   America—India—Israel   74

CHAPTER 5   Political Theorist   100

CHAPTER 6   Chairman of the Labour Party   120

CHAPTER 7   Action for Libel   140

CHAPTER 8   Family Man   156

Index   171

To my wife
Elizabeth

FOREWORD

BY THE
RT. HON. JAMES CALLAGHAN
M.P.

10, DOWNING STREET,
LONDON, S.W.1.

I am very grateful to Granville Eastwood for allowing me to introduce his new book about Harold Laski, a man whose writings and speeches influenced so many of us during the Thirties and Forties. What emerges in these pages is Laski's erudition, his capacity for making the written word live, his brilliant speeches, his unceasing work, his devotion to the Labour Party, and, most attractive of his many qualities, his kindness to countless young students and his willingness to go the extra mile to help them. During the last thirty years whenever I have travelled to America, to India or to almost any part of what is now called the Third World, at some stage I was bound to meet a distinguished academic, administrator or politician who would boast that they had been taught by Laski when they were young students at the London School of Economics. It was almost as if there was a brotherhood of such people scattered throughout the world and his indirect influence on their countries has been enormous. He did not confine his kindness and consideration to university students as I have personal reason to know. I was a young trade union official in the Thirties and Douglas Houghton, the General Secretary of the Inland Revenue Staff Federation allowed me to take to the Arbitration Court on my own responsibility a dispute for settlement. Harold Laski was one of the three members of the Court. I knew his reputation well and as a young man naturally stood in some awe of him. He listened carefully whilst I presented both the written and the oral evidence and after the Award had been made I was surprised to receive a letter from him in his well known tiny hand-writing asking me to visit him at the London School of Economics. There in his study he told me I should read for a degree, but I declined saying that I was too busy with my trade union and Labour Party work. He did not give up and instead made arrangements with the Librarian at the London School of Economics for me to read there whenever I wished and gave me an open invitation to go and talk to him. Unfortunately I did not take enough opportunity of either offer. But Laski did not forget me and a few years later he joined with John Parker to recommend me to Transport House as a potential Parliamentary candidate. I knew from this and other incidents that he was kindness itself.

I had discovered Laski's "Grammar of Politics" some years earlier. I believe it was the first serious work of political theory that I read and I can still remember the excitement as his ideas, new to me, tumbled out of their pages. For weeks I carried it with me, reading it on the bus and in my lunch break until I had devoured every word. I wanted to discuss it with people I met and was naively astonished to find that my contemporaries were not as interested as I was. I dare say that nearly fifty years later it appears dated to the present day reader but at that time it was like opening up a new continent for me.

Granville Eastwood reports the views of some people that Laski's reputation as an academic suffered because of his political work. This may well be so but speaking as one who as a young man listened to him in the 1930s I can only say that I am glad that he was so active politically in the Labour Party for his speeches up and down the country influenced a far wider circle than he could have done if he had confined himself to the London School of Economics.

After 1945 Harold Laski never seemed to recover his old verve following his notorious libel case and his tussle with Clem Attlee, but it was a tragedy that ill health and over work caused his death at an early age in 1950. I like to believe that in his later years and in the more reflective mood that was settling on him he could have produced yet more books of the same high quality as those he had written when he was a young man. I am grateful that this book will recall Harold Laski to the present generation. He deserves to be remembered and I hope that young people may still find in his books and in his conception of political theory something of value to inspire them in the never-ending march of democratic socialism.

AUTHOR'S NOTE

I am greatly indebted to Mr H. L. Beales and Mr Gordon Brunton for their encouragement, especially during the early days of the project and to Professor Julius Lewin for his invaluable guidance and advice as the book progressed. I deeply appreciate, too, the most helpful way in which Mrs Frida Laski talked to me about her late husband.

It is not practical to mention here all those in this country, the United States and elsewhere who, by their memories of Harold Laski, enabled me to give what I hope is a balanced portrait of him. I trust that the inclusion of their recollections in the pages which follow will be accepted as acknowledgement of my indebtedness to them.

I am very grateful to Sir Max Aitken for the ready way in which he placed at my disposal the *Daily Express* book of the Laski libel action. My thanks are due to the librarians and staffs of the London School of Economics, the Labour Party and *The Times* for their assistance.

It is especially gratifying to me that, amidst all the pressures of office of Prime Minister, Mr. Callaghan readily agreed to write a Foreword.

CHAPTER ONE

EARLY DAYS IN ENGLAND AND NORTH AMERICA

I once heard Harold Laski say to a gathering of young trade unionists: 'I was born with a silver spoon in my mouth and I advise you all, if you have the opportunity, to do the same.' He was always conscious that, by the fortunate accident of birth, he had had a better start in life than most people and this showed itself in his desire to help those who were experiencing difficulties in efforts to educate themselves or embark on a career. He never forgot how fortunate he had been in his own early days.

Harold Joseph Laski—to give him his full name—was born in Manchester on 30 June 1893, the second son of Nathan Laski, a wealthy cotton shipping merchant, and his wife, Sarah Frankenstein Laski. His father had been brought to this country as a baby when his parents, Naphtali and Esther Laski, came to England from Poland. They lived in Hull for a time, later moving to Manchester, where young Nathan obtained employment as office boy in a shipping firm mainly engaged in trade with India. A member of the family to whom I am indebted for some of these details told me with pride how, over the years, Nathan Laski gained the confidence of his business associates, rising to be head of his firm and a prominent figure in the public life of Manchester. A Liberal in politics, he became a magistrate and was a leader of the city's Jewry for well over thirty years, his appointments including the chairmanships of Manchester Jewish Council, Jewish Hospital and Jewish Board of Guardians.

But whilst Nathan Laski was a strong personality in business and civic life many stories have been told to illustrate the influence of his wife over the family and home. There was the occasion when they went to a meeting in the city's Library Theatre with its strict ban on smoking. Nathan Laski, puffing merrily at his cigar, ignored the chief librarian when, very politely, he drew his attention to the rules of the theatre. However, knowing how things stood, the librarian gently mentioned the matter to Mrs Laski. When her husband commented 'I've nearly finished it' his wife declared 'Nathan, put that cigar out at once' and the order was promptly obeyed.

Nathan and Sarah Laski, with their three children—there was a daughter and two boys—lived in the Cheetham Hill district of Manchester. At that time it was an almost exclusively Jewish residential area with synagogues catering for the various degrees of orthodoxy. Their substantial yellow-brick house—Smedley House—is still standing although many of the neighbouring houses have long since been demolished and the whole district has drastically altered. There were those who thought that the Laskis, when they had consolidated their obviously satisfactory position, might have left Cheetham Hill and moved to a more fashionable district of Manchester but they chose to remain where—many years earlier—they had settled down and their children had been brought up. In a word, they felt comfortable and 'at home'. Theirs was an orthodox Jewish household with strict attention to Jewish dietary laws and observance of the sabbath and other holy days. The children were taught Hebrew at an early age.

Some idea of Nathan Laski's standing in the Liberal Party in the city may be gained from the fact that when, in 1908, Winston Churchill fought a vital Parliamentary by-election in the West Manchester constituency he stayed with the Laskis at Smedley House. In after years Harold Laski liked to tell how, during the campaign, Churchill used to sit on his bed and talk to him. At that time Churchill was Member of Parliament for the constituency and when Asquith succeeded to the Premiership he appointed him President of the Board of Trade with a seat in the Cabinet. He therefore had, as was required in those days, to submit himself for re-election, and in the event was defeated. Soon afterwards, however, he found a fresh seat at Dundee. Churchill could never have imagined as he chatted to the fifteen-year-old boy at Smedley House that the day would come, nearly forty years later, when he would use him as a bogey-man in a general election which would sweep the Labour Party to absolute power at Westminster for the first time.

Although politically poles apart, Harold Laski and Churchill kept in touch over the years, and when Nathan Laski died in 1941 Churchill, then war-time Prime Minister with tremendous burdens on his shoulders, found time to write to him about his father, saying: 'He was a man whose heart overflowed with human feeling and whose energies were tirelessly used for other people and large causes. I feel I have lost a friend and all my memories of Manchester and Cheetham are veiled in mourning.'

Laski (from now on I propose, with a few exceptions, to use only the surname when referring to the subject of this book) started his formal education at a private school in the city and from there went to Manchester Grammar School. The headmaster at that time was John Lewis Paton who, during the twenty years he was there, gave full scope to his genius for personal influence over boys. It was said he never forgot a name or a face and he soon began to take a close interest in Laski. In later years he was extremely proud to have had him as a pupil, as he was of William Temple when, before coming to Manchester, Paton had been a master at Rugby School.

Although for some years after he left Manchester in 1924, Paton worked in Canada, becoming president of the Memorial University College in St John's, Newfoundland, he maintained contact with Laski, and after returning to England in the late 1930s, they met on odd occasions to talk over old times and exchange views on educational developments. Many people urged Paton to write his memoirs and reproduce some of the correspondence he had had with 'old boys' of the various schools with which he had been associated but he remained the most unassuming of men. He declined to sit for his portrait and destroyed his personal papers to ensure the fulfilment of his wish that no biography of him should be written. It was said that the only memorial he wanted was the influence he had had on the boys whose good fortune it had been to come in his care. Laski certainly never forgot him. Whilst he was a brilliant pupil, Laski's Manchester schooldays were marred by bouts of illness, he at one time being bedfast for almost a year. However, he needed no encouragement by either his parents or teachers to make good use of these periods of enforced rest. Books were his constant companions.

At the end of 1910 Laski won a scholarship to New College,

Oxford, and his father generously decided that his son should not take the emolument and would therefore be an honorary exhibitioner. The result of this was that the student next on the list who would otherwise have been unable to go to Oxford received the grant. About that time Laski became keenly interested in eugenics —we shall see one of the reasons a little later—and having made certain of a place at Oxford he left Manchester and spent the next six months studying the subject under Karl Pearson at University College, London.

Laski's interest in eugenics was such that he had an article accepted by the *Westminster Review* and this caught the eye of Sir Francis Galton whose study of heredity led him to the conviction that the human race might gain an indefinite improvement by breeding from the best and restricting the offspring of the worst. To this he gave the name of 'eugenics'. Then eighty-eight years old, ailing and with only six months to live, Galton recorded in his diary on 11 July 1910 that he had been in correspondence with the writer of the article and had that morning learned 'that he is a schoolboy from Manchester, aged seventeen. It is a long time since I have been so much astonished. The lad probably has a great future before him and he will make his mark if he sticks to eugenics which he says has been his passion for two years. I as yet know nothing more about him but I hope to learn'.

Shortly afterwards they met and Galton recorded in his diary: 'My wonderful boy Jew, Laski by name, came here with his brother to tea. The boy is simply beautiful. He is perfectly nice and quiet in his manner. Many prodigies fail but this one seems to have stamina and purpose and is not excitable so he ought to make his mark.' A few months later Galton was dead and out of his ample estate he made provision for the foundation of a chair in eugenics in the University of London, making it known that he wished Karl Pearson, with whom Laski was studying, to be the first professor.

Going up to Oxford in mid-1911, a major decision by Laski, after a year's study, was to change his subject from science to history, and in June 1914, having worked tremendously hard, he was placed in the first class of the honours list in modern history. He also won the Beit Memorial Prize offered annually for an essay on some subject connected with colonial history or with the advantage of imperial citizenship.

During all this time Laski's private life was being subjected to stresses and strains the outcome of which affected his whole future. At Christmas 1909, at the age of sixteen and whilst still at Manchester Grammar School, he went to a party at Halesowen, not far from Birmingham, having been to a convalescent home there some time before whilst recovering from an operation for appendicitis. There he met Frida Kerry, the twenty-four-year-old daughter of Francis John Kerry, a farmer and landowner of Acton Hall, Suffolk. A lecturer in eugenics and living at Earlswood (also near Birmingham), she was a trained physiotherapist who had studied in Sweden and taught in Belgium. Laski was fascinated by Frida Kerry's talk and when he returned to Manchester after the Christmas holiday he enthusiastically set about interesting himself in eugenics. The two corresponded regularly over the months that followed and met again by mutual arrangement from time to time.

In mid-1911 they decided to marry, Frida Kerry having in the meantime taken up employment as a lecturer in Glasgow, and when, after much heart searching, she told her parents, they strongly disapproved of their daughter marrying an eighteen-year-old Jewish boy still to embark on his studies at Oxford. In an effort to put a stop to it they threatened to tell Laski's parents what was afoot, and so, without more ado, the young couple decided to get married at once and went to Glasgow where they could become man and wife without the consent of Laski's parents.

The ceremony over, the newly-weds told their families what had happened and although they knew the Laski family would be sorely hurt they could hardly have imagined the strength of the opposition to their son marrying a Gentile. Nathan Laski at once became ill and took to his bed. Whilst writing this chapter I had a talk with Harold Laski's widow (a few weeks after her ninetieth birthday) about those days and she recalled, along with her husband, being visited by a Laski relative and taken to Smedley House where Harold was immediately shut up in a room at the top of the house. Frida Laski was at once put to bed and the wedding-ring taken from her finger.

However, although the marriage was a most grievous blow to Nathan and Sarah Laski's religion and family pride (they had always taken it for granted that their son would marry a girl of

Jewish faith in their station of life) there was in fact little they could do about it. In due course Frida Laski went back to her lecturing post in Glasgow and Harold Laski was watched over closely at Smedley House until he was released to begin his new life at Oxford. His parents gave him a modest allowance to cover his Oxford years and he was told that if he persisted in his marriage there would be no further financial assistance unless his wife adopted the Jewish faith. The Laski family insisted that the marriage was to remain a secret and that Frida Laski was to continue her work in Scotland and remain separated from her husband. The family strongly opposed reunions, which they learned later were taking place at very infrequent intervals in Glasgow during vacations, and the young couple only met twice in Oxford during the three years Harold Laski was at New College. However, his parents could not prevent the exchange of letters, and Laski tried to ease the heartache of their enforced separation by writing to his wife twice every day during term.

During one of the talks I had with Mrs Laski whilst I was writing this book she gave me an unpublished manuscript which her husband had written at the time of their marriage. It was clearly intended to be considered a fictional piece of writing but it seems reasonable to assume that what he wrote was influenced by his own experience and may well have been set down as the type of letter Laski wrote to his father and the kind of correspondence that followed from it. However, of one thing we may be sure. Laski felt, even in those very early days of his marriage, that he could not imagine life without his wife by his side.

The manuscript which Mrs Laski gave me tells the story of a young Jew who married a Gentile older than himself and was aware, of course, of the 'fierce hatred of his race for intermarriage'. In the course of a letter to his father, telling him that he has married outside the faith, the young husband says:

> Because I know how greatly this news will hurt you, I want to tell you firstly all that I feel, to ask you to understand, and if forgiveness be needed, to forgive because you understand. And first let me ask you to believe that I have done this with no conscious desire to hurt you. The old love is not altered, nay, rather enriched by the new. I seem to understand things so much more rightly, to realise more vividly, all you have done for me. It is of the woman who taught me this that I would tell you. . . .

After telling how they met and how much they meant to each other in the early days of their friendship, the young Jewish husband's letter to his father goes on:

> The more I saw of her soul the more could I rejoice in its delicate purity. I rejoiced, too, in the wonderful sympathy she could give. I was not physically strong and yet always she made me feel that physique was nothing so long as there was the desire of the spirit and an eagerness for the highest.... I bring you my wife as one who, I am certain, will but serve to increase the ties that bind us together. I want you to feel that because she is of a creed different from your own that our love is not a sinful thing. She has my ideals. She appreciates the faith I hold. If that be a faith different from that which you have taught me to love, if, as I think, it is a faith wider and less dogmatic, so purely an intellectual difference will surely in no way strain the intimacy of our relationship. You see I place great hopes in your answer to me. I believe that because I am your son you will forgive me for running counter to your most dear convictions. The creed I hold cannot admit that the marriage between Jew and Gentile is a sin.... I shall be a Jew because there is a Jewish race; not a Jew because I believe in the literal observance of the tenets of Judaism. I feel, too, that holding this keenly as I do, it would be folly and dishonesty on my part were I to hide from you what I have come to see....

But the father's reply to his son shattered all hopes the young husband may have held. He was told:

> You are no longer my son. You have chosen to run counter and wilfully counter to the belief which you were aware was dearest of all to me. What crime have I committed that my son should thus throw overboard the faith I and my Fathers have held for countless generations. Is the stainlessness of our history nothing to you. Do you hold so cheaply that great rabbinic tradition of which my family has been so long and so rightly proud.... In return for the care and attention that have always been lavished on you, you do the one thing which to us is unpardonable.... For your mother's sake I am willing to receive you as my son, even to acknowledge your wife, if you on your side will undertake the fulfilment of certain fundamental conditions. Your wife must adopt the Jewish faith. She must promise to observe it as your mother observes it, literally and with a heart full of love and esteem for the ritual.... And you will further pledge yourself to bring up your children to a wholehearted belief in the truth of Judaism. I require further that you make no open

acknowledgement of your marriage until your wife has been received into the Jewish Church; to do so would be a fatal blow to the social prestige of our family which I shall assume you are unwilling to do. On these terms I am willing to allow time to heal the wound you have thought it a light thing to inflict. Otherwise let there be an end to our kinship.

In reply, the young husband tells his father:

If I say that your letter has filled me with sadness perhaps you will understand that to me words seem both futile and inadequate. I have read and re-read your letter; have tried to read into it a little of the old confidence and the old love—yet with a heart that yearns to do so I cannot. I see only a demand on your side that I should surrender convictions that I cherish as deeply as you esteem your own faith because it is my misfortune to think differently. I see an assertion that to search after one's own happiness is cruel. I see affection proffered on terms of dishonour to myself,—terms that impugn the sincerity of my belief as they would destroy the freedom of my soul. I had hoped, it seems vainly, that you would appreciate my assertion that this difference between us, since it is a difference of opinion merely that can in no way influence personal conduct and private emotions need not compromise our personal relations.

It seems to me that I cannot honourably accept the conditions of relationship you would wish to impose. Firstly and chiefly, I cannot ask my wife to subject herself to an intellectual servitude which would be as galling to her to endure as it would be for me to inflict. I cannot consent to force upon her a belief in which at the outset she has no confidence.... Nor would it be moral on my part to bring up my children in a faith which seems to me to have no meaning for today. I wish to leave them free to choose by the light of their own thought and their own experience. I cannot either consent to keep secret the fact of my marriage. To do so would mean a tacit admission that there was in it something disgraceful that I wished to hide from general knowledge. To my mind it is not so branded,—rather am I proud and glad that so glorious a woman has given me the privilege of her most intimate confidence.

The reply of the young husband to his father concludes:

How much it hurts me to write you this I cannot adequately tell you. I wanted so much to feel that this new world of love did not mean the destruction but rather the extension of the old. You have willed it otherwise, and, under the conditions, I can do no more than accept your decision. Yet it seems to me that you are only intensifying the tragedy of the Jew, only making bitter his awakening. I ask you to consider whether two thousand years of persecution ought not to have made us lovers of liberty. Upon the fundamental conceptions of Judaism it is not for me to attempt your conversion. But I would remind you that in all things the spirit rather than the letter must count; and with the modern Jew it is becoming a sacrifice of the substance to the shadow. There is no persecution so bitter as that which comes from one's own friends; no misunderstanding so tragic as that which they force upon you. So for the present our paths must lie apart; yet perhaps one day they will meet, and we shall all go forward on the same road together.

Whilst working hard at Oxford (he had to cram three years' study of history into two years because of his change of subject) Laski took an active part in university life. He played tennis, was a regular attender at the debates of the Union Society and was an especially enthusiastic supporter of a New College debating society called the Twenty Club where he did most of his practising as a speaker. Years later he said he went to Oxford with radical views, that his years there confirmed him in them and that his debt to the University was immeasurable. His keenness for eugenics was such that he formed a Galton Club and he was also a member of the Fabian Society. Towards the end of his time at Oxford Laski was a supporter of the suffragette movement, as was Frida Laski in Glasgow, both mainly restricting their activities to the more constitutional forms of campaigning. Indeed it was Laski's association with the suffragettes that brought him into contact with George Lansbury who, in London, was editing the *Daily Herald*—when Laski finished his finals at Oxford in June 1914. Years later Laski said that 'contact with Lansbury was a great education. He was absolutely straightforward, absolutely democratic and entirely fearless. Through him I got my first chance of seeing the inside of the socialist movement, and at a critical time'.

Impressed with Laski's personality and breadth of knowledge, Lansbury offered him a summer months' engagement as a leader-writer on the *Daily Herald* and this brought the Laskis to London and living together under the same roof for the first time. Mrs Laski has told me how happy they were in a house just outside London lent by Lady De La Warr, a well-known suffragette and friend of Lansbury. 'My husband used to travel to the city by train', Mrs Laski said, 'and it was wonderful to have each other's company part of every day.'

Immediately on the outbreak of war in August 1914 Laski tried to enlist in the armed forces but was rejected as medically unfit for military service. The modest allowance from his family had come to an end on his leaving Oxford and it was imperative that he should find regular work. He was wondering what he should do when he was approached by the Warden of New College, Oxford, and asked if he would like to go to McGill University in Montreal (it had been founded in 1821 through a bequest of James McGill, a prominent citizen) as Lecturer in History. It was explained that the vacancy had occurred because G. N. Clarke, who had accepted the lectureship, wished to be released from his obligation to go to McGill so that he could join the army and permission would not be granted until he had found a replacement.

'The invitation to go to Canada seemed a wonderful opportunity', Mrs Laski told me. 'Our relations with the Laski family were very low—they had commented scathingly on my husband writing for the *Daily Herald*—and after talking things over we decided to accept. McGill University was to pay our fares on arrival, and on condition that we refunded the money, Harold's father bought us our travel tickets. And so in September we sailed for Canada. When we arrived at McGill there was a telegram awaiting us,—it was from Nathan Laski asking for the immediate return of the passage money.'

As you would expect, Mrs Laski has many memories of those far-off days. 'Although there were times when we were lonely, it was all a great adventure', she has said, 'but clouded by our straitened financial circumstances.' Watching the progress of the war in Europe, Laski tried to join the Canadian armed forces when it was clear that it was not to be 'over in twelve months' as most people predicted, but again he was rejected on medical grounds.

Laski and his wife continued to share each other's interests and he was soon inviting his students to their Montreal home for informal evening talks, something unheard of before at McGill. In this way there began a practice that was to become a feature of Laski's academic life for the many years ahead. Also during this time he started to develop his remarkable facility for writing and in his first year at McGill he had two magazine articles published. They were 'The Means and the End' which appeared in the *New*

Republic and 'The Personality of the State' published in *The Nation*.

Anxious to encourage adult education amongst the workers in Montreal, Laski was active in the establishment of a branch of the Workers' Educational Association, and once a week a group of men and women gathered at his home to study history and politics. Laski never lost his early enthusiasm for the WEA and in later years, when he was fully established at the London School of Economics, he was always willing, often at considerable inconvenience, to give talks to small groups of members as well as address larger gatherings organised by the Association. 'If they are ready', he once said, 'to devote some of their limited leisure to study after they've done a day's work I ought to be willing to do what I can to help them. They deserve all the encouragement they can get.'

Needing to supplement his income, Laski turned his hand to a wide variety of literary commissions some of which took him over the border into the United States. Mrs Laski recalled to me an occasion in the spring of 1915 when they were passing through New York, and a railway porter, discovering that they were British, asked them very earnestly if they were on their way home. If they were, he said, he advised them not to travel by the *Lusitania* as the Germans were going to sink it. Laski told his inquirer that they were remaining in North America and thought no more about the incident until, a few days later, on 5 May, came the news that the Cunard liner had been sunk off the Irish coast by a German submarine with the loss of twelve hundred lives. 'That night', Mrs Laski said, 'we were having a meal in a New York restaurant when the sound of great jollification came from an adjoining room. When we asked what it was all about we were told that it was a party of Germans who were celebrating the sinking.'

It was whilst he was in Montreal that Laski made the acquaintance of Felix Frankfurter, then a young professor at the Harvard Law School and later to become a distinguished Justice of the United States Supreme Court with a great reputation for intellectual integrity and judicial mindedness. Frankfurter had heard about Laski through the editor of *Harper's Magazine* who said he had met 'the most extraordinary fellow I've ever come across anywhere' at McGill. Frankfurter was so intrigued by what he was told that when he next had need to go to Canada he went out of his way to visit McGill, and the resultant meeting was the beginning of a friendship that lasted until Laski's death well over thirty years later.

Frankfurter was so impressed with Laski that when he returned to Harvard after their meeting he suggested to the Dean of the Graduate School there that he would be an asset to the teaching staff. Mrs Laski has recalled how full of enthusiasm her husband was for an appointment there when he returned to Montreal from a brief visit to Harvard in mid-1915. And all this time the Laskis were financially embarrassed (their rent being a particular strain) and Laski reminded the Principal of McGill he had promised that, after a period, his salary would be increased from 1,500 dollars to 2,000 dollars. 'Have you the promise in writing?' he was asked, and when he said it was a verbal assurance he was told that no notice could be taken of that. However, when in January 1916, Laski told the authorities at McGill that he was leaving, having been appointed Instructor in History and Tutor in the Division of History, Government and Economics at Harvard, he was at once assured that, if he stayed, his salary would be immediately increased. 'It's too late', Laski said, 'I'm leaving.' During the months between his Harvard appointment and taking up his new duties the Laskis' only child Diana was born (on 27 May, surrounded by medical students in a Montreal hospital) and to meet his soaring expenses Laski undertook considerable extra work including visits to New York to write for the *New Republic*. There was one occasion when Laski had to choose between paying a doctor's bill or the rent. Then he remembered that he had an etching of Seymour Haden's in London and he at once wrote home asking for it to be sold and the proceeds telegraphed to him.

In the summer of 1916, whilst waiting to assume his Harvard appointment, Laski was taken by his friend Felix Frankfurter to Beverly Farms, about thirty miles from Boston, to call—at his summer home—on Mr Justice Holmes, a member of the United States Supreme Court and son of Oliver Wendell Holmes, the distinguished writer and author, amongst many other books, of *The Autocrat of the Breakfast Table*. It was a momentous occasion for them both. Laski was a young man of twenty-three and Holmes a national figure in his early seventies. When he got back home Laski wrote a brief letter of thanks to which Holmes sent a longer acknowledgement and in that small way there started a correspondence between the two men that was to span almost twenty years and continue until Holmes died in 1935. Each kept the other's letters (they were all handwritten) and after their deaths they were published by the Harvard University Press in two large volumes spanning over 1,400 pages. From time to time we shall see what they had to say to each other. Although the two writers differed fundamentally on many issues they maintained throughout a high level of intellectual regard for each other whether they were corresponding on history, philosophy, political theory, law or family matters.

Laski took up his duties at Harvard on 1 September and before long the home they were getting together was much more adequately furnished than when they had first settled in. He told Holmes: 'We are having an immensely happy time here. For the first time since I left Oxford we are pretty free from financial cares and though we can't yet buy books still we can draw up the lists of them ready for the time when I blossom into a full professorship.' It is clear from his letters of those days that Laski was proud to be associated with Harvard University, America's oldest institution of high learning (it was formed by John Harvard in 1636) and situated at Cambridge, near Boston, in Massachusetts.

Laski was soon on the way to winning the hearts as well as stimulating the minds of his pupils, and, recalling those Harvard days for me, Lucille Harrington said that, as a Roman Catholic, she often clashed with Laski during a course of lectures dealing with the Reformation. 'There were many opportunities for disagreement', she told me, 'but to his everlasting credit he respected my right to hold views contrary to his own and encouraged their expression. "Come on Miss Harrington, I love to fight" he would say and he did. On papers which revealed convictions contrary to his he gave me the highest mark, adding "I am in complete disagreement!" All my life I have been grateful to him for the stimulus of his teaching. As a Catholic I did far more reading of the great Catholic historians than I otherwise would have in order to be ready to meet the challenge of debates with him.'

Laski's arrival at Harvard coincided with a desire on the part of the authorities there for the reorganisation of the system of teaching. The methods of Cambridge and Oxford were being studied and adopted by American universities, and Laski, of course, was quite familiar with the tutorial system of teaching with pupils coming to their tutor's room either singly or in small groups for advice on the course of their work and to bring exercises and essays for his criticism. Myer Israel, then a Harvard student and now a Boston lawyer, told me, 'the tutorial system which Laski helped so much to introduce was new to Harvard but it certainly worked'.

During his early days at Harvard Laski combined study for a degree at the Law School with his teaching duties and although he found the task too much he maintained an interest in the subject and amongst articles he had published in the *Harvard Law Review* was 'Liability of Charitable Corporations for Tort'. Another, 'The Personality of Associations' was later reprinted in his book, *The Foundations of Sovereignty*. Before long he was helping, as book editor, in the preparation of the *Harvard Law Review*, difficulties of war-time publication being accentuated by a depleted staff because of the calls of military service.

The year 1917 is also a landmark in Laski's career for another reason. It saw the publication by the Yale University Press in the United States and by the Oxford University Press in Britain of his first major work, *Studies in the Problems of Sovereignty*. It ranks, in the view of many, as one of the author's 'Big Four'. It was also during his Harvard days that Laski started to develop his passion for book collecting, beginning to build up a library that in later years was to become one of his most cherished possessions.

There is plenty of evidence that, right from the early days of academic life, Laski had the urge to give practical help to his students as well as do all he could to further their education. Richard L. Strout, a journalist on *The Christian Science Monitor* for thirty years, is one of several who has told me of his own student days at Harvard. Like others, he has talked of taking tea with the Laskis at their home, and he also told me, on deciding to go to England, of being given letters of introduction to C. P. Scott (editor of the then *Manchester Guardian*) and to Laski's parents in Manchester, and of being given advice as to what he should do to launch himself in journalism in England. 'I owe the greatest of debts to Harold Laski', Strout told me. He went on, 'more than any other teacher I had I really felt he was interested in me as an individual, and when—years after he left Harvard—

I called on Professor Laski at his London home he recognised me at once and made me very welcome'.

The practice which Laski started at McGill of inviting students to his home soon developed into a much-commented-upon feature of his Harvard life. One student of those days told me that he wrote in his diary for Sunday, 28 September 1918, 'went to Mr Laski's to tea. A memorable experience'. Another commented to me: 'When Mr Laski opened his house as well as his office to those he was teaching it was a most unusual occurrence at Harvard where, at that time, there was a sharp separation of students from faculty. With his wife and baby daughter by his side it was all very novel and exciting to us.' Much later Laski was to say that his years on the American continent were the most fundamental of his life; he learned that it was his vocation to be a teacher.

Laski's popularity with his students did not endear him to some of his Harvard teaching associates and he became aware that other reasons for their attitude towards him were his self-assurance and the fact that he was a Jew. He sensed that anti-semitism was one of the reasons for a teaching colleague, Sheffer, too, being out of favour with the authorities (he had also married someone they did not approve of) and Laski was so anxious to remove the prejudice against his associate, who taught in the Philosophy Department, that he wrote home to England enlisting the assistance of Bertrand Russell who had indicated in his *Introduction to Mathematical Logic* that he thought well of Sheffer. 'Do you know anyone at Harvard well enough to say (if you so think) that Sheffer should have a chance?' he wrote, saying that he was sure a word from Russell in support would carry weight with Lowell, President of the University. Russell, without delay, did his best to help and succeeded in his object.

At that time both Laski and his wife took a great interest in the theories and writings of Leon Duguit, French jurist and law professor at the University of Bordeaux, and—working together—they translated from the French one of his major works on political pluralism, *Law in the Modern State*. They were so pleased with the outcome of their efforts that they sent copies of the book, published in 1919 in New York, to friends at home.

During the second half of 1919 a situation developed that ultimately led to the Laskis deciding to leave the United States and return home to England. It happened like this. After very prolonged efforts to secure better working conditions and unsuccessful attempts to have a bona fide trade union recognised by the authorities, the police in Boston withdrew their labour as a protest against low wages and long hours of work. Before a volunteer force was called into action there was some rioting and looting in the streets of the city, and troops were used amidst vigorous demands for the protection of property and life.

The story of the Boston Police Strike, as it was called, has its place in the saga of those days of industrial unrest in America. It is a complicated tale with the men being dissatisfied with their method of organisation and seeking to form a genuine trade union, and Police Commissioner Curtis charging and sentencing those who were considered to be the leaders of the campaign. There had been abortive attempts over a considerable period—including a mayoral investigation—to find a compromise solution to a situation that had been festering for years, and one can see, reading the record, that the men lost patience and decided to take action. The newspapers said of the strike that Boston was facing up to a 'Red dictatorship', that it was 'an attempt to overthrow Americanism' and a 'skirmish with bolshevism', and amongst those who responded to an appeal to the citizens of Boston to take the places of the strikers were over four hundred from near-by Harvard University; indeed its president, Lowell, offered the services of the University to the city immediately the dispute started.

It was in this atmosphere, in mid-October, and after the dispute had lasted for over a month, that Laski addressed a meeting of the wives of the striking policemen. The newspapers gave considerable coverage to his speech in which he strongly attacked the handling of the situation by Commissioner of Police Curtis. He said he was lacking in statesmanship, had failed in his duty to protect the public, and showed no real knowledge of his duties. The police had been described as deserters, Laski said, but it was the Commissioner who was the deserter, refusing at any time to consider the men's grievances. He said the people of Boston were waking up to the fact that twelve hundred men could not be entirely wrong. Labour, he declared, was more united than ever and would never surrender.

Laski was attacked for his speech on public platforms as well as in the Press, references being made to his being an alien and a

Jew. Fellow teachers at the University were amongst those who strongly disapproved of his intervening ('interfering' they called it) in an industrial dispute, and in a letter to Bertrand Russell, Laski wrote: 'I spoke for the striking police here the other day; one of those strikes which makes one equally wonder at the endurance of the men and the unimaginative stupidity of the officials. Two newspapers and two hundred alumini demanded my dismissal. I was charged with teaching sovietism when I said that men who get 1,100 dollars and work a seventy-three hours week are justified in striking after thirteen years' agitation.' One newspaper asked if Laski was 'an instructor in or a lecturer upon American government or Soviet government' and commented 'the parents of the sons entrusted to his tutelage are entitled to know'. There were suggestions that he should be sent back to England. A more sober comment made at the time by a public figure was: 'The friends of Mr Laski will feel that they are serving both him and the college if they remind him that a sense of propriety and good judgement are important ingredients in an intellectual make-up. I am one of those who share President Lowell's opinion that freedom of speech should be encouraged and that a muzzling policy is contrary to the best interests of a university. I am sure you will agree with me, however, that there are restraints which a right-minded and loyal instructor should impose upon himself, especially at a time like this.'

A special edition of the satirical Harvard *Lampoon* was published, making a scurrilous attack on Laski, in order, it said 'to expose this propagandist in our midst'. The flaming red cover of the magazine depicted Laski as a Socialist saint. Another drawing showed the Socialist Day of Judgement with Laski surrounded by human freaks casting better-dressed citizens into the outer darkness. Harvard students were exhorted to 'stamp out this spark of bolshevik propaganda' and amongst many other abusive contributions was a violently anti-semitic cartoon.

No action was taken by Harvard University President Lowell in spite of pressure from many quarters. A Harvard student of those days told me that it was known at the time that Lowell had no use for Laski's views but that he defended his right to maintain and express them. Laski said later that the President spoke with kindness but explained with emphasis that a teacher limited his utility when he took sides on matters of current controversy.

Lowell is understood to have expressed the view privately that Laski 'did a noble job for academic freedom'. 'Lowell', Laski told Bertrand Russell, 'does believe in free speech so that I stay—but you can get some index to the present American state of mind.'

Looking back to those days, Mrs Laski has recalled how deeply her husband was wounded by the attacks and how it unsettled them both. Since they had arrived in North America five years before, Laski had worked hard both at McGill and Harvard and was beginning to build up a reputation in the academic world as a scholar and teacher. By his writings he had become known far outside the confines of Harvard and he had felt that henceforth his career was assured. Both he and his wife, had, until this happened, been happy, and they were sad to think that a passionate belief in individual liberty and free speech and a well-intentioned desire to help the under-dog had led to their situation. And, whilst he had not been dismissed from his teaching post, Laski came to the firm conclusion that he could not hope for advancement at Harvard.

Although he put a brave front on it all and had acquired a love for the United States that was to be strengthened as the years went by, Laski was temporarily disillusioned, and early in 1920 he made it known that he was eager to 'get away from this country' but was uncertain how to do it. He said he had no hope in Oxford, that he knew no one in Cambridge, and was placing his hopes on something turning up in London where he knew that Graham Wallas, then Professor of Political Science at the London School of Economics, was doing what he could to help. Two governors of the School, Sidney Webb and Viscount Haldane, also used their influence on Laski's behalf, and the School's Director, Sir William Beveridge, decided, as he later put it, 'to rescue him from an uncomfortable position at Harvard'.

Apart from the atmosphere at Harvard there were other reasons why Laski was pleased to be returning to England. It would, as he put it, 'bring Frida within range of her own people' (her parents had got over their daughter's marriage) and he told his American friend Holmes:

The position offers me £700 a year, an amount of teaching very much less than I now do, colleagueship of men who are the real masters of my subject, and, above all, England.... I have looked at it from the personal angle of Frida and my own people and the conclusion is that I ought not, personally or intellectually, to refuse it. . . . The School is above all the place where I have been anxious to teach. I can lecture there on the subjects about which I care most and the work is almost entirely with graduate students. Then I have at hand the prospect of political work with the British Museum and the Public Record Office from materials nowhere else available. The income is not as large as I have here but the time occupied in teaching leaves me a good deal more freedom both for books and such work as I have done these last four years in the *New Republic*.

He added that his friend Felix Frankfurter, and Lowell, the Harvard principal 'both emphasise their belief that the post is for my work ideal. I feel that, too'.

And so, on 22 June 1920, Harold and Frida Laski, with their four-year-old daughter, sailed for England, to take up duties at the School where he was to spend the next thirty years.

CHAPTER TWO

TEACHER AND FRIEND

Shortly after arriving back in England Laski wrote to his American friend Justice Holmes to say that 'merely to see London again was too lyrical an experience at first for sane committal to paper'. He said that his appointment to a lectureship at the School was 'precisely what I wanted' and although they were to be at variance later, he spoke of Sir William Beveridge, Director of the School, as 'a charming fellow with all the qualities of the best type of civil servant'. Very early on Laski made friends with Graham Wallas whom he was later to succeed as Professor of Political Science at the School, describing him as 'an eminently lovable person'.

Laski was very soon in a wide mainstream of affairs, briefing himself as to what was happening in politics and the academic world. He lunched with men like H. W. Massingham (the journalist and critic who edited *The Nation*), C. F. Masterman (its literary critic) and H. N. Brailsford, a well-known journalist who helped to give his readers in the *Manchester Guardian* and elsewhere an informed understanding of political affairs. Before long Laski himself was writing for *The Nation* and other journals and he lost no time in renewing his friendship with Beatrice and Sidney Webb, the latter then Professor of Public Administration at the School. He frequently listened to debates in the House of Commons, met and talked with Parliamentarians and political commentators with the result that he soon felt able to take a full part in discussing affairs of the day. Amongst others he was on terms of personal friendship with was Lord Haldane, ex-War Minister, who was soon to become Lord Chancellor in the first Labour Government.

Less than a month after his return Laski was telling Holmes:

I went to Manchester and saw my people for the first time in nine years. I went because I thought I ought to show them that there was a real eagerness on my part for the resumption of our relationship. I don't think it did any good. They've become very wealthy and my income and prospects are not on the plane which interests them greatly. And since I am finding it impossible to rent a house and cannot buy one under £3,000, and since they must give us the £3,000 as I don't possess it I am afraid we'll have to live in St James' Park until they feel that Frida and Diana can be palatable even though they were not born Jews. Do you mind if I consign all religions to eternal damnation?

A week later Laski wrote to Holmes that he had 'found a delicious little house' in South Kensington, 40 Onslow Gardens. He added that 'my father came out a trump, for though he won't come to see us and persists in regarding my marriage as a crime and Diana as an illegitimate child, he offered to pay for the furniture with the result that the house is supremely comfortable. I wish you could see it. I never dreamed that buying furniture could be so poetic,—yet so it is. The real triumph is the dining-room, which is all Chippendale'.

At the beginning of November, Laski was writing to Holmes:

After negotiations that were as agonising as they were absurd my family and I have made up the ancient quarrel. Largely it's due to Frida's common sense and courage and their amazing perception that I don't give a damn for their money and had therefore better be left to my own vicious views and a penniless career. The result is that my father has gone to India happier than he has been for years, full of almost extravagant delight in Frida and me, and with copies of my books in his trunk that he may talk to me of them when he comes back. It's all very pathetic; for nine years ago the same thing could have happened if he had cared for it. The main thing is that he feels happy though puzzled at my refusal to accept £1,000 a year from him; puzzled I suppose, on the theory that no son of a business-man ought to live up to his principles. I'm very glad over it all for it brings Frida into her own.

There seems to be some uncertainty as to just what happened to bring about the change of heart on the part of the Laski family. Probably there was more than one reason. It has been said that Frida Laski went through the formalities required to become a member of the Jewish community but when writing this book I asked her, during one of our talks at her London home, just how I should describe what took place. After some thought she said to me: 'Just say that I made myself agreeable to my husband's family. I'd like you to leave it at that.'

Of course, in the nine years that had passed since the marriage in 1911, Laski's parents had seen their son become established in the academic world. He had done extremely well at Oxford, was the author of books and articles that had been well received on both sides of the Atlantic, had an assured position at the London School of Economics, and his prospects for advancement were excellent. During the last days of 1920 Laski wrote to his friend Maurice Firuski, who kept a bookshop he used to frequent when at Harvard:

This week, by the way, we have been almost engulfed by my mother, brother and sister whose welcome has been so eager to us that we don't know whether we're on our heads or heels. I don't think, Maurice, that we were unwise to be generous; first because it's never unwise to be generous and next because the friends they have, about whom I care, are now convinced that the blame rested on my people from the start,—a reason for which I was very anxious.

Early in the New Year Laski wrote again to his American friend and, during the course of his letter, said: 'We all went to Manchester for four days a fortnight ago. I wish you could have seen it, Maurice. We were treated like gods, with a deference and politeness quite beyond words.'

Laski took up his new duties as lecturer at the London School of Economics in October 1920 and I have had the opportunity of making the acquaintance of a considerable number of those who were his students at the School during his thirty years there. He seems, right from the start, to have developed a style of speaking that left a lasting impression on all who heard him. Slight of figure, with his smooth black hair parted down the middle and wearing large spectacles, he stood rather stiffly, almost at attention as he spoke, and with expressionless face, totally devoid of the gestures of emphasis that are part of the make-up of many speakers. Ken Gay, a former student has told me how, with the lecture-room very often crowded and with students standing at the back to hear him, Laski seemed at times 'like a mature school boy but one went in awe of his encyclopaedic knowledge. His strong personality always came through. He was rather egotistic in attitude but he was greatly liked and indeed admired'. Formally dressed in a three-piece suit and tasteful necktie (and wearing a dark Homburg hat in the street) it was commented that Laski's appearance suggested a middle-class accountant or banker. Beatrice Webb said he was 'just a trifle too smart for a professor of socialist opinions'.

Another student of those days, P. R. Crowe, now Emeritus Professor of Geography at Manchester University, told me:

A little man would slip rapidly and unobtrusively along the School corridor, whistling to himself and noticing nobody. He entered the lecture-room and, as soon as he had closed the door, he would start to speak with exceptional clarity and in a slightly abrasive and faintly Americanised tone. There was never a note and rarely a pause. Whole paragraphs of various authorities were quoted from memory, verbatim, without a trace of hesitation and only a slight change of tone. Yet soon there would be a reference to yesterday's news, to the recent comment of a prominent political figure or industrialist to illustrate a point. When he introduced a wisecrack there was barely time for a chuckle, never time for a real laugh. There we sat, anxiously awaiting the next turn in the relentless argument. Nobody was spared but one always felt that, with Laski in full cry, if the current victim had been present in the lecture-room, he, too, would have been chuckling at the sparkling wit and complete lack of ill-feeling. Exactly at the end of the fifty minutes period the lecture came to an end. There never happened to be the slightest difficulty about this; it always ended sweetly, rounded off perfectly with almost astronomical precision. And, turning swiftly, he departed, maybe whistling, from the room.

Ralph Miliband, now Professor of Politics at the University of Leeds, has said, recalling his student days at the School:

Professor Laski would begin to speak in that odd accent of his, an inimitable accent that everyone tried to imitate, carving out long and involved sentences, yet somehow clear and precise. I only heard him once lose himself in an intricate metaphor and he stopped short and said 'Now, how do I get out of this sentence' and he laughed as heartily as any of us. His moods would change as he went on, sometimes serious and earnest, sometimes merry and irreverent; and he loved the laughter that echoed round the hall at an epigram or artfully built up story. Yet, underneath all he said, there was ever present the passionate conviction that what men had thought mattered, that the answers they had given to the problems of their time had meaning for us, and that their blindness, no less than their wisdom, held lessons; that we in this hall were engaged in a fine adventure of evocation. And his mastery of his science, his knowledge of its every nook and cranny, made him as penetrating in the dissection of the implications of Civil Service reform as of Rousseau's general will. No subject with which he dealt could be dull and no audience could fail to come alive at his contact. It is good to think that for generations of students, the years at the School are bound up with his memory, that the thought of Harold causes so many of us to recapture the years when the world was young and we thought, as he once told me, half approvingly, half warningly, that 'we had caught truth by the hair!' His lectures taught more, much more, than political science. They taught a faith that ideas mattered, that knowledge was important and its pursuit exciting.

Many other people to whom I have spoken about Laski's style of lecturing have referred to the enormous length of many of his sentences. They have told me, as they listened, fascinated by his fluency and polished eloquence, sometimes they felt sure he would never be able grammatically to complete a sentence. But almost always, in the end, with apparent effortlessness, he got himself out of the maze and all was well. It almost seemed that, on occasions, he did it quite deliberately to show the remarkable agility of his mind. Laski's photographic memory and his tremendous reserves of nervous energy also impressed those who came in contact with him. Kingsley Martin, at one time an assistant of Laski's at the School, said that the first time he met him he was 'stunned by his brilliance'.

In his day-to-day teaching of politics Laski never lost an opportunity to make it very clear that he did not pretend to be impartial in the views he put forward to his students. He firmly held that to try to do so was an impossible objective and, if pursued, would only result in a teacher destroying his personality. He always emphasised that what he presented to his students was the truth as he himself saw it and when he submitted his conclusions on an issue he was at pains to explain how he had arrived at them and that it was for his listeners to make up their own minds on the problems raised. Laski knew that his views on the issues he dealt with were well known to his students as a result of activities outside the lecture-room and he felt he could not be a different person in the world outside from what he was when he was in the

School. He held the view that to be honest and straightforward was the only way to win and hold his students' confidence.

Laski developed this point in the course of his Inaugural Address at the School on 26 October 1926 to mark his appointment to the Chair of Political Science. Saying 'we do not ask in this university the acceptance of any political creed' he went on:

> My object as the occupant of this chair is not to create a body of disciples who shall go forth to preach the particular and peculiar doctrines I happen to hold. It is rather that the student shall learn the method of testing his own faith against the only solid criterion we know—the experience of mankind. That does not, of course, mean that in the exposition of political philosophy it is one's business to pretend to impartiality. In any case that is impossible; for in the merest selection of material to be considered there is already implied a judgement which reflects, however unconsciously, the inevitable bias that each of us will bring. The teacher's function, as I conceive it, is less to avoid his bias than consciously to assert its presence and to warn his hearers against it; above all, to be open-minded about the difficulties it involves and honest in his attempt to meet them. For the greatest thing he can, after all, teach is the lesson of conscious sincerity. More truth is discovered along that road than can be found on any other.

Turning to the subject again in his address, which was given to a crowded and widely representative audience, he said:

> I know no place where, as I believe, social problems can be better or more fitly studied than within the walls of a university. We can introduce there, as we cannot in the conflicts of the market-place, the doubts and hesitations, the quantitative estimates, the limited certainties, that necessarily appertain to all solutions. I am tempted to argue that while statesmen, who have to convince vast multitudes, must necessarily live by purveying undistributed middles, the student in an academic atmosphere has a unique opportunity of examining creeds and hypotheses in entire indifference to the results of his examination. He can take questions like the right of private property, the limits of toleration, the sovereignty of the state, and examine them as a zoologist examines his specimens in a laboratory. And he must teach what he believes to be the results of his inquiry so long as he is careful to base those results upon the widest induction that is open to him, and with an insistence upon the large margin of probable error which attaches to all social theorems.

When Laski had finished his address there was an immediate

request that what he had said should be placed on permanent record. One who was present has told me how impressed his hearers were and there can be no better way of indicating the way in which the newly-appointed professor approached his new responsibilities than to quote his peroration. He ended:

Our civilisation is being tested by a strain as great as ever led to the destruction of past empires. Its margins are haunted by the conflict of races, the struggle of classes, the clash of colour. If we are in the end to survive, we must, above all things, bend our energies to the discovery of knowledge. There is no other road to salvation. We are not less destined than our forefathers to earn our livelihood in the sweat of our brow. We have, do not let us forget, the overwhelming task of giving to the common man that access to his inheritance of which he has hitherto been deprived. He tests our effort not by the thought and pain that have gone into its making so much as by the results it achieves. He remembers not its fragility, but its power. We have to discover both what he wants and how, with justice and wisdom, we may meet those wants. Only as we posses that knowledge can we await his judgement with confidence.

I do not, believe me, minimise the difficulty of the task. I realise full well how little we shall ever know, compared to what we desire to understand. I am, I hope, only too dismally aware to how few of us it will be given to account our achievement either significant or rare. Yet I have some measure of confidence. The highest of all joys, after all, perhaps because it is the most difficult, is the effort to show the connection between the facts one studies and the structure of the universe. The very difficulty of our problems only makes the pursuit more ardent and the results more precious.

That pursuit, moreover, is conducted here in an atmosphere peculiarly suitable to the task. This School is old enough to have a tradition and young enough to have avoided dogmas. It works in an atmosphere that is eager only that inquiry should be made, and regardless of, even if it be interested in, the conclusions of the inquiry. As a laboratory of investigation it is very happily placed. The libraries are at our elbow; the great departments of State, the House of Commons, the government of London, can be observed and analysed at first hand. May I add that I, particularly, am fortunate in a body of colleagues who make the work of teaching and research less a labour than a privilege? In the years that lie ahead we shall seek additions to knowledge as worthy as we can make them of the trust that has been confided to us. We shall do that, not with the thought or hope of impressing upon our students any special doctrines or convictions, but, as we desire, with the power to live their lives more fully by reason of the ferment created in them. It is our ambition to inspire in them a silent devotion to the great subject we serve. We are still young enough to believe that the service of thought is the noblest calling to which a man can devote himself. We ask to be judged by the measure of our effort to make others think likewise.

Paul Nash, a former student at the School and now of Boston University, told me that one day Laski was lecturing in the Old Theatre in the School and the acoustics were abominable. A brash young student who was sitting under the balcony stood up and called out: 'Professor Laski, could you speak a bit louder, we can't hear you.' Laski, Nash said, never paused for a moment in his speech or altered his tone or volume in any way. All he intoned was 'Listen harder . . .' and he went on with his lecture.

I have been impressed, whilst writing these pages, by the very considerable number of men and women who have shown an obvious desire to pay tribute to their former teacher, anxious that I should do justice to the memory of a man who helped them so much during the formative years of their lives. When one remembers that it is over a quarter of a century since Laski died and that some who have discussed him with me were looking back nearly fifty years, it is the measure of the debt of gratitude they owe to him. All I can do is to pass on the feelings and memories of just a few.

Warren Dahlstron, an American who was a student of Laski's at the School, comparing his teachers there with one another said:

I had a philosophy course with K. R. Popper who glorified Socrates. Laski was Socrates. He seemed to bring an element of poetry to political thinking. A touch of Mid-Western protestant evangelism of the very human and loving kind,—not logically precise necessarily but warm and inviting.

Rupert Emerson, now Professor Emeritus at Harvard University, also gave me a warm picture of Laski who was his tutor at Harvard and later at the School. He told me:

Laski's knowledge of the obscure was to me most extraordinary. I remember occasions when he was reading the latest chapter of a dissertation I had written I would mention with pride my discovery of some unknown German figure of, say, 1787. He would acknowledge that my discovery was a legitimate one but ask me if I knew a more obscure figure of, say 1774 and his predecessor of 1753. When, later, I looked them up I found that they actually existed. How Laski could have known about them or remembered them on the instant I cannot conceive.

Edward Littlejohn, now a business executive in New York, told me that in 1934 he left his native Australia and the University of Sydney for the London School of Economics where he came under Laski's influence. After leaving London he settled in the United States and recalled for me that one day he was waiting at traffic lights to cross a busy New York street when he heard someone call out his name. Littlejohn went on:

It was Harold Laski. I had not seen him for five years and he couldn't have known that I was in America. But he not only recognised me and recalled my name but came across the street and asked me a number of searching questions that clearly showed he also remembered the course of study I had pursued years before under his guidance. It was uncanny and made a big impression on me at the time.

Shirley Adelson Siegel, now an Assistant Attorney General of the State of New York, recalled for me how the course of her life was changed by Laski's insistence, when she was about to leave the London School of Economics, that she should apply to Yale Law School rather than enter Columbia Law School as she intended. She told me:

When I protested that the date for applications was passed—and that besides that I lacked the fifty dollars that had to accompany the application—Professor Laski dismissed my objections with a wave of the hand. He promptly dictated a letter, in my presence, to the registrar at Yale urging that my application be considered—almost as a personal favour—in spite of the lateness of the date. He enclosed with the letter to the registrar his personal cheque for the fifty dollars. The choice of Yale in preference to Columbia was so right for me and just what I needed.

During my time at the School I had a particular interest in the field of housing and slum clearance and Professor Laski put me in touch with officials in the Borough of Fulham where he lived and where, I believe, his wife was a Borough Councillor. I had a marvellous opportunity to observe first hand, hearings on condemnation and redevelopment plans and accompanying inspectors. This provided grist for papers not only in Professor Laski's class but for other courses I was concerned with as well.

The door of his office at the School was always open to those of us from America and Canada. A few years later, when I was at Yale, Professor Laski visited the University and, in effect, summoned me to his presence, to inquire how my studies were progressing. That was the last time I saw him.

Samuel Rezneck, now Professor Emeritus of History, and living in retirement in his native America, recalled for me the days as a pupil of Laski. He said:

I look back on the three years I was favoured with Laski's interest and influence as perhaps the most formative of my life. It was not only his ideas, expressed so brilliantly, but the warmth of his nature and personal relations that gave depth and meaning to his influence. I remember him as I remember no other of my teachers. This is a testament to Laski as a decent human being not merely as a teacher and ideologue. The last in particular has been much criticised in later years but the basic character of the man is beyond and above criticism.

John Hutchinson, now Visiting Professor of International Relations at the Johns Hopkins University in Washington, DC, said to me, of Laski:

How lovely it was to have known him. I have never known students anywhere in the world look upon a teacher with such affection and eagerness as his students looked upon him. I have never known anyone who improved the quality of mind and propensity of those around him as he did. As the days grow shorter I do not remember anyone I have been happier to know.

It all started for me when I was an evening student at the London School of Economics but the combination of a full-time job, evening study and poor food in 'digs' was such that I either had to quit my studies or become a full-time student. Laski hardly knew me from Adam but intervened with the Minister responsible for Education to grant leave of absence for lowly Executive Officers in the Civil Service.... I got leave, the first, I think, ever granted to anyone of my rank in the Service. It was for a year and a half, and it changed my life. Later Laski was instrumental in my coming to the United States but that is another story.... He was a great teacher if by that we mean a man who can bring a great subject alive and induce students to devote their happy best to wrestling with the issues he raised. He was too, an incredibly generous man, both with his time and money. He could inspire in the sense that you could enter his office defeated by an intellectual problem and leave it feeling that you were at least potentially the greatest living authority on the subject. He was the kind of man who left a permanent presence.

As just an example of Laski's patience and anxiety to be fair here is an incident related to me by another United States student at the School, Wellman J. Warner. He said:

One day Laski came to me about one of my fellow students from the United States who had written a dissertation. After a careful reading Laski told the student that he could not approve the manuscript. The student's brash response was that what he had submitted was so original that Laski couldn't grasp the import of what he was saying. Laski, as faculty supervisor, could have retorted, 'That's my decision' and ended the affair. Instead he replied, 'If you want me to I'll appoint the usual authority outside the faculty to sit on your examining committee and we will go along with his decision!' I seem to recall that the man selected was from Oxford. In any event, that professor came back to Laski and reported that he would approve the dissertation if Laski asked him but if he did he wanted it understood that he would never consent to sit on another doctoral committee in Political Science at the London School of Economics. Of course, the dissertation was disapproved.

Mrs Jean Herbert, now resident in the Channel Islands, told me:

As a naïve social science diploma student from Manchester at the School I had never seen anyone like Professor Laski. In lectures he made bitingly intolerant references to capitalists and all their works and I felt then that he was unduly biased. Altogether, he seemed a very frightening and sarcastic person. I should explain that my father was opposed to the whole idea of the London School of Economics, declaring that he would meet my expenses only if I agreed to study at Manchester or Liverpool. But I was twenty-four; I went to London just the same, applied for a grant and took with me all my savings, just over £100, which seemed a small fortune to me. After a few months I found that even with the most frugal living, my savings were dwindling with alarming rapidity and no grant appeared. I began to turn over in my mind all kinds of schemes for earning ready cash. My pride would not allow me to ask my father for help. Finally, I confided my difficulties to a fellow student. To my astonishment he suggested that the most sensible course would be to go along and have a chat with Professor Laski. A day or two later I felt desperate enough to do just that. The man I met in his study was a complete contrast to the restless, accusing figure in the lecture theatre. A kindly smile transformed his face as he listened patiently to the halting tale of my plight. Then he picked up the telephone and the conversation went something like this. 'Ellen' (the Minister of Education was Ellen Wilkinson), 'I have a student with me who has financial worries due to delay in receiving her grant and this is undoubtedly affecting her work. Would you just see to it for me, there's a dear.' I stammered my thanks and stumbled out, quite overcome by an eminent man's concern for the troubles of an obscure student and the knowledge that I was the subject of a personal plea to the Minister of Education. To my great relief the grant arrived three days later. From then on, Professor Laski was a shining saint in my eyes. I learnt, too, the injustice of making superficial judgements on a person.

When Benjamin Lippincott, now of the Department of Political Science of the University of Minnesota, recalled for me his memories of Laski he was, like many others, looking back well over forty years but the passage of time has done nothing to diminish his gratitude for one whom he described as 'the most inspiring teacher I ever had'. After telling me about his earlier days at the London School of Economics, Lippincott said:

At graduate level he considered you something like a colleague, albeit a junior one. Here, in a one-to-one relationship you had even more opportunity to present your views yet you were still open to instruction which, on occasion, could be quite drastic. I shall never forget the time when I first brought in a chapter of a work that later became *Victorian Critics of Democracy*. In the draft I submitted to Laski I had quite unconsciously taken on in my writing some of the rhetorical language of the Victorians. Laski returned the chapter a few days later with one word written on the margin of two different pages; the word was 'horrible'! I blanched and he said: 'Lippincott, write your own style.'

Lippincott told me that he spent a great deal of time during the next few weeks studying to improve his style. He went on:

I returned to Laski some three months later with another chapter of the book and went to his office the following week not without fear and trepidation, wondering what bomb-shell he would drop this time. He handed back the chapter and, on quickly turning over the pages I could find no comment of any kind. I asked him if the chapter was satisfactory. Laski replied, 'Lippincott, I am writing one of the presses in America to get ready for your book'. I was quite stunned. I thanked him and left hurriedly, running practically all the way to the nearest postal station where I cabled the family 'Going into teaching'. Although I had set my heart on becoming a correspondent for a liberal journal in the United States I now found that I could no longer be happy in journalism. My brief exposure to a life of scholarship at Oxford and London, along with the personal encouragement of Laski, rendered me unable to settle for anything less than a try at an academic career.

Victorian Critics of Democracy was, in due course, published in the United States—and dedicated to Laski—and was the first of several books Lippincott wrote during a distinguished academic life.

E. T. Steer, a student at the School said, after sketching a picture of Laski in the lecture-room:

What a contrast with that impression I received when he became my adviser of studies in a later year and I used to visit him in his room to discuss essays I had written on subjects set by him. At these discussions he was invariably friendly and full of encouragement. If he considered my literary style could be improved he would select a work by someone he regarded as a master of English from the book-lined walls and read out a passage to illustrate his point. If he thought further reading around the subject of the essay would be useful he would select an appropriate volume for me to take home.

One of the things that has impressed me whilst I have been delving into the breadth of Laski's activities has been how readily he put himself at the disposal of his associates. The American student, Warner, I have already referred to, said to me:

May I give you an example of Laski's kindness whilst I was at the London School of Economics. Although Hobhouse was my supervisor in working up my study of Religion in the Industrial Revolution, Harold Laski had read it in manuscript and offered his criticisms and suggestions. After the Dissertation Committee's approval I had signed a contract with Longman's, Green, for its publication, and was not only returning to the United States but to distant California for a lengthy stay. Laski came to me and said, 'It is going to be an arduous and lengthy job for you to see this book through the press from so far away. Let me read the proofs and take care of the publishing routines for you.' I never saw a proof of the volume. He carried it through to publication. A busy man of world-wide stature and he gave without stint this time and attention to take the burden off the shoulders of one of his students. That was the warmth, the kindness and the humility of the man as I knew him.

In 1923, when there was nothing like the nation-wide facilities for blood transfusion there are today, Laski had what he described in a letter to Holmes as 'a queer experience which has involved three weeks' cessation from work. I have a German student who, as you can imagine, has been persistently undernourished for some years. He took ill with pernicious anaemia and the doctors decided that it was a case for transfusion. The poor fellow hadn't, of course, a relative in this country, so I naturally volunteered and a pint of my blood now flows in German veins. It was a most queer business. For about a week it left me as weak as a cat; then a fortnight of quite glorious lethargy, when gazing at the ceiling seemed work. Now I'm on the job again and as fit as can be'.

Laski adds that while in bed recovering 'of course I could read' and I have heard many people comment on the almost incredible speed with which he could take in the contents of a book. He once wrote to Holmes:

Of books I have had a long dose, owing to three days in bed. It began with novels, none good except the old ones, and moved forward to a better line of thought. I re-read Trevelyan on Italy and, to my astonishment, found a large part of it merely brilliant rhetoric where ten years ago I remember being swept off my feet by it. I read a great book on the Indian government reforms by Lionel Curtis called *Dyarchy* and with pride I affirm and do take my oath to the fact that I read the whole six volumes of Masson's *Life of Milton* with great pleasure. And I re-read Morley's *Cromwell* with a little envy, easily the best summary of the man, though one feels Morley's sententiousness a little trying at times. And these modernities were rounded off by River's *Instinct and the Unconscious*, a real masterpiece, and B. Russell's *Theory and Practice of Bolshevism* which I felt to be a great contribution as a piece of analysis.

On the outbreak of war in September 1939 the Ministry of Economic Warfare took over the University buildings in Houghton Street and arrangements were made for School to be evacuated to Cambridge. It will be readily appreciated that this put considerable additional strain on Laski who, because of his London commitments, was not able to take up permanent residence in Cambridge. Instead, he used to make the journey from London regularly, and Ralph Miliband, a student of those days and now Professor of Politics at the University of Leeds, has recalled:

> I like to remember him in the early days of the war when the School was in Cambridge. He would arrive every week from London and come straight to School from the station. The winter was bitter and trains unheated. He would appear in his blue overcoat and grotesquely shaped black hat, his cheeks blue with cold, teeth chattering, and queue up with the rest of us for a cup of foul but hot coffee, go up to a seminar room, crack a joke at the gathering of students who were waiting for him, sit down, light a cigarette and plunge into controversy and argument; and a dreary stuffy room would come to life and there would only be a group of people bent on the elucidation of ideas. We did not feel overwhelmed by his knowledge and learning, and we did not feel so because he did not know the meaning of condescension. We never felt compelled to agree with him because it was so obvious that he loved a good fight and did not hide behind his years of experience. He was not impatient or bored or superciliously amused. A seminar was a place where one could talk back. He was involved; part of the argument, hard hitting, sometimes angry, sometimes even unfair. At least he took us seriously, and it was good for us that he did. He was concerned with explaining, making complex thoughts simple, correcting a fact, helping to formulate an idea someone felt deeply yet could not quite express. Sometimes this would go too far, and Laski would interrupt and say, 'What you mean is...' only to be told that that was not it at all, and there would be a burst of laughter and he would relapse into temporary silence. His seminars taught tolerance, the willingness to listen although one disagreed, the value of ideas being confronted. And it was all immense fun, an exciting game that had meaning, and it was also a sieve of ideas, a gymnastic of the mind carried on with vigour and directed unobtrusively with superb craftsmanship.

Continuing his memories of those days, and making the point that in spite of all the problems associated with war-time travel, temporary accommodation, food rationing, and bouts of ill-health, Laski continued to take a deep personal interest in his students, Miliband said:

> I like to remember Harold, too, in his personal relations with students. He devoted an enormous part of his time to them; he had infinite patience in dealing with their problems, all their problems, academic and personal, and the distinction was a ludicrous one so far as he was concerned. His interest in students continued to be

wide enough to include anyone who went to see him, whether he knew him or not, whether promising or dull. Laski suffered fools, not gladly, but patiently in the hope that he could help to make them less foolish. It often puzzled me, this almost indiscriminate willingness to see and help anyone who needed help. I think I know now why he gave himself so freely. Partly it was because he was so human and warm and that he was interested in people. But mainly it was because he loved students, and he loved students because they were young. Because he had a glowing faith that youth was generous and alive, eager and enthusiastic and fresh. That by helping young people he was helping the future and bringing nearer that brave new world in which he so passionately believed. 'Youth is hope' he would say and it made little difference that he was often disappointed, and that he would grow older and less keen. Every new year was a challenge, and every new season brought its promise.

Laski was a frail man, often ill, very often in pain. During one whole term he paid weekly visits to his dentist and came back to teach, a little pale and wan, a little apologetic for not being quite himself. A man much more robust would have been exhausted by a programme of work that encompassed a thousand different interests.

Recalling those days, H. L. Beales, then Reader in Economic History at the School, has said, 'he was so heavily committed to the service both of the School and of his political responsibilities that his vitality was overtaxed. I remember, for example, walking with him to Mill Lane lecture-rooms when the School was in Cambridge, his impedimenta in my cycle-basket because I doubted if his strength was equal to carrying them'.

Norman MacKenzie, now Director of the School of Education at Sussex University, was a student of Laski's at the School during the war years. He recalled for me that, when a course was finishing, grateful students contributed to a special and most unusual kind of writing-board which Laski could use whilst—as was usual—writing in an easy chair, and MacKenzie was deputed to make the presentation one day when they were all gathered in the common room. 'When I had finished my little speech', MacKenzie told me, 'Laski said "thank you" in a perfunctory sort of way and never mentioned the matter again all evening. We were, of course, a little disappointed but a day or two later I had occasion to see Laski and, referring to the presentation ceremony, he said he hoped he hadn't been thought ungrateful but he had been too overcome at the time to say anything.'

I talked to MacKenzie about those Cambridge days whilst I was at Brighton—where he now lives—for a TUC conference, and he needed no encouragement to look down Memory Lane and stress how strenuously Laski worked during the war years. To enable evening students to continue their studies the School retained a branch in London for a time and during this period— it lasted about a year— Laski taught his principal courses both in the capital and at Cambridge. When the air-raids began in London the premises there were closed but it meant no lessening of travel for Laski who continued to spend part of his week in London—as I shall relate, I met him on one of those occasions—as well as going around the country. His Fulham home was damaged during an air-raid and although evacuees from the East End were billeted in his Essex cottage at Little Bardfield he looked forward tremendously to spending odd week-ends there. In the course of our talk MacKenzie said he could not do better than refer me to a piece he wrote about the war years (and which Kingsley Martin used in his memoir of Laski) in the course of which he said:

... The burden that he bore in these years, however, was not merely physical. Wartime conditions made academic life arduous even in Cambridge, and his schedule was always crowded. He was one of a very small number of professors who were with the school throughout the war without interruption. Some of his colleagues were in ministries; some were on special assignments; others were on war service. Of all the members of the school's Government department, certainly, he was the only one who taught continuously, and in the absence of the others he had to carry an additional load of teaching if something like a full course was to be offered. True, the classes were smaller, but it takes as much effort to deliver a lecture to six as to sixty or six hundred. This work he regarded as his main war work. His standing as a politician made it virtually impossible for him to take even a temporary Civil Service post, for he was too partisan a figure to be hidden quietly away in some routine job. And his criticisms of the Coalition and especially of Winston Churchill were sharp enough, after the first flush of enthusiasm and optimism of 1940 had died down, to make him unpopular with the Cabinet figures who chose the men for the kind of special assignment which alone someone in Harold's position was able to take. War work for Harold, then, was of a special kind; it was both to help maintain civilian and military morale; to keep, through his syndicated articles in the American press, opinion in the United States alert to the English and European changes and vicissitudes; and through his teaching, to equip his students to face the problems that would come their way in the aftermath of war. Allied to his political work, in more senses than one, was his tireless round of military hospitals, RAF stations, Army camps, and the like, lecturing, taking part in brains trusts and all that proliferation of Forces Education which took place in the years before the invasion of Europe. Often, not surprisingly, the officer or sergeant in charge of such activities would turn out to be an LSE graduate and one of Harold's own students. I can think offhand of six or seven such occasions. There must have been many more. Such visits and talks not only served as a release for Harold's own passionate hope than an anti-fascist war would mean positive victory for democracy; they also kept him in close touch with the way an articulate minority of the Forces was thinking. He would go back to Cambridge or Little Bardfield, where he would spend his weekends, full of enthusiasm for the spirit of the men and women he had met on these visits, often equipped with a new anecdote, but sometimes aware of a rankling grievance that officialdom had overlooked or of an example of gross waste or inefficiency. And he would sit down and write to an MP or a minister, or to the department responsible, or to the Prime Minister himself. He became, to adapt a phrase of his own, a kind of walking delegate for the trade union of ideas....

Looking back it seems remarkable that Laski managed to keep going at all. He worked himself so incessantly that he had a serious nervous breakdown in 1943. MacKenzie, who recalls calling on him in his Cambridge rooms when he had 'not for the first time had a black-out and fallen downstairs', concludes his review of the Cambridge years:

... Those who were Harold's students during these years, I believe, formed unusually close personal ties with him. In the first place, they were few enough in number to permit him to know each of them intimately. Secondly, he was as conscious as they were that time and the war's demands pressed upon them and he did his best to give them the kind of encouragement, the talk and the insights, that he could give so abundantly and superlatively. They responded by a deep and abiding affection for him. Only those who have taught know the wrench that a university teacher feels, even in normal times, when his graduating class parts from him. The war gave a special edge to that feeling for Harold and it brought it more frequently and bitterly as each year the school was stripped of young men for a war which Harold could fight only vicariously. He gave many of them the sense that they knew for what they were fighting; they, in turn, renewed his hope that this wartime generation would help to find a world better than that of 1918–1939 in which they had grown up. For Harold, it was one of those experiences that moved him beyond speech when students, on going overseas, told him that, should they be killed, it was to him that they had told their wives to turn immediately. There can be no greater compliment to a university teacher than that.

Otto Kahn-Freund, formerly Professor of Comparative Law at the University of Oxford, has said how Laski helped and sustained him during one of the most anxious periods of his life. Early in May 1940 Kahn-Freund was chatting with colleagues at the School (where he was on the staff) when he saw a headline in a friend's evening newspaper 'Hitler Nearing Channel Ports'. He told me:

I felt shattered. My wife and I, because we are Jews, had sought refuge in England when Hitler came to power in Germany, and now it seemed inevitable that the Nazis would catch up with us. I felt so distressed that, without a word to anybody, I left the group and went upstairs to my room. A few minutes later there was a knock on the door and when I called 'come in' Laski entered. 'I could see you were despondent downstairs', he said, 'and I readily guessed the reason. I've come up to tell you not to be depressed. Maybe you don't know the British people very well, and perhaps you think that Adolf Hitler is going to have an easy passage across the Channel. You may be sure that we shall put up a tremendous fight and I am confident we shall hold out. So, please, don't worry.' Those few words of Laski's gave me new life and hope. I shall never forget his thoughtfulness in leaving his friends and seeking me out to reassure me at a time when I was terribly depressed.

George Wolf, now Professor of Physiological Chemistry at the Massachusetts Institute of Technology, related to me how he came to England from Austria as a Jewish refugee child. Matriculating in 1940 he was anxious to become a full-time science student but needed financial support. Failing to get help from various organisations, he happened to attend a Laski lecture whilst the School was at Cambridge and spoke to him afterwards in the common-room at Trinity College there. Wolf told me: 'Laski listened to my story attentively and with sympathy but with few words and simply said he would help me.' Next Wolf heard from a relative of Laski's who was in charge of a Refugee Children's Movement and she offered to support him to the extent of £2 a week until he obtained his BSc. 'That', he said, 'was enough for me to live on in those days and I had a scholarship at Queen Mary College—London University—to pay the fees. I graduated in chemistry and physiology in 1944 and found my own support to do research and obtain the DPhil from Oxford in 1947. If I have had a reasonably successful career in biochemistry since, I owe it initially to Professor Laski's unquestioning and immediate readiness to be of help.'

I myself had an example, during the war years, of Laski's eagerness to help people in a sphere completely outside the academic world whilst I was living in my native Lancashire. In 1941 I applied for a post in the Research Department of the Labour Party at their headquarters in London and was invited to Transport House for an interview where I appeared, with others, before a sub-committee consisting of Hugh Dalton (then a member of the Churchill Government), Laski and the then General Secretary of the Labour Party, James Middleton. Towards the end of my interview I was asked what my position was regarding national service and I explained that as a full-time trade union area secretary I was in a reserved occupation. It was then explained to me that the staffs of political organisations (as different from those on the industrial side) were not exempt from national service and that if I was given the post I would cease to be 'reserved' and liable for call-up. 'As a matter of fact', Dalton said, 'the vacancy we are seeking to fill has been caused because a young man has been called up and if we appoint you we should be liable to lose you in the same way and have to start filling the vacancy all over again.'

This, of course, meant the end of my being considered for the vacancy and when the interviews were over I was leaving Transport House when Laski came down the stairs in a great hurry—brief-case under his arm—presumably dashing off to keep another appointment. However, when he saw me he stopped and—as if he had all the time in the world—Laski took me on one side. 'Look here, Eastwood', he said, 'I am sorry the way things turned out for you this morning but I hope you won't be too disappointed. I'm sure something will come along for you before long and when it does you may be glad you missed this job.' His parting words were: 'Don't worry, everything will probably turn out all right.' And then he suddenly became a man in a great hurry and dashed into the street. Laski's friendliness was just what I needed and his comments proved very sound. Later I was elected Assistant General Secretary of the Printing and Kindred Trades Federation, eventually succeeding to the position of General Secretary.

A social science student at the School just after the war and when it had returned to London, now Mrs Yvonne Craig, has recalled for me how she developed 'a lasting affection and high regard for Harold Laski' and after paying tribute to his 'stimulating lectures impeccably styled and magnificent in the richness of their content' she said:

My own evolving Socialism (although always strongly differentiating from his because of my Christian beliefs) was inspired by his teaching and passion for justice to all men. I have one story that may interest you. We members of the student Christian Movement, Christian Union and other Christian Societies at the School had successfully petitioned and protested until we were given a small room for worship, meditation and private prayer. We equipped it ourselves, had it consecrated for Holy Communion, and used it regularly. This, of course, was very offensive to Harold Laski who regarded the LSE as a temple of secularism. He knew he could say nothing to prejudice a minority cause—as we then were—so he craftily adopted another technique for ridding the School of the unwholesome presence of a chapel. He took to visiting it over a period of time, carefully noting the numbers of people using it in order to present a statistical analysis which would persuade the Students' Union that the room could be more effectively used for certain cramped tutorials.

Alas, I left the School as battle was about to be enjoined and I believe that, in the end, Harold Laski won. During this post-war period the creative intellectual life of the School was at its height, in my opinion, and this was reflected in the deep spiritual and political debates which went on between the Christians and the Marxists. In fact the School had probably the first formal Christian Marxist Study Group when members of both orientations joined together for collective action on social issues such as refugee work in Europe and reconstruction projects at home.

Professor George Lanyi, of the Department of Government at Oberlin College, Ohio, told me:

There was one aspect to Harold Laski which cannot be enough appreciated. He was very kind to students and had an intuitive genius in advising and helping them in difficult situations. He hardly knew me as a student except as his daughter's friend. I graduated from the London School of Economics in the summer of 1937 after which I returned to my native Hungary to join the staff of my father's newspaper. In the spring of 1938 Hitler invaded Austria. Having learned in London to see the world from a wider perspective than it was the custom in my small, native country, I was absolutely convinced that this was merely the first step towards a successful conquest of Eastern Europe by Hitler. I doubted that Britain and France would be able or willing to prevent him from initiating such a venture. Quite unwilling to live under a Hitler-Hungary I wondered where to turn with my young wife. I took a short vacation, went to London to obtain advice from teachers and friends. Europe in those days was divided by rigidly-guarded frontiers and legal immigration from one country to another was incredibly difficult. Immigration to England, for instance, was, for me, well nigh impossible. Nor did I have the slightest idea what I would do, once a resident in England. From my earliest youth I had planned to become a Hungarian newspaperman. Thus I was not a particularly ambitious student, an academic career was not what I wanted. Once in London, in May 1938, I was rather disappointed at being unable to obtain any sort of advice. Some said that I should try to stay in Hungary and simply flee the country once things had become much worse. Laski's daughter, Diana, was the only one who was optimistic; she directed me to her father with the encouraging remark 'Dad *always* has suggestions'. So I stumbled into Laski's study at the School and told him, in a few sentences, my tale. He looked at me for a minute or two and then asked me: 'Can your father sustain you for about two years in America?' I said I thought that might be possible. 'Then I'll tell you what to do. You go and study International Relations at Harvard. Americans are not very good at that sort of thing. Europeans have great advantage over them. After all, you are interested in politics and you have all sorts of experiences in it. I will write to President Conant of Harvard. After two years in America you will stand on your own feet. Everybody does in that country.' He wrote to Conant, Harvard admitted me, my father managed to finance my first two years there, and afterwards I managed quite well on my own. Arriving in New York in December 1938 I called on Laski, then a Visiting Professor at Columbia University. He was delighted to see me and immediately sat down and wrote two letters to friends of his in the Harvard Government Department, Merle Fainsod and

Rupert Emerson. Both received me most kindly, became my teachers, and later, close friends.

Mrs Vera Derer, *née* Lewisohn, Laski's personal secretary at the School for two years shortly before he died has spoken of his consideration for his personal staff and of his anxiety not to inconvenience them because of his calls on their time as a result of his many activities. Often away from his room at the School, he would find it necessary to write making requests for books and papers, for travel arrangements to be made, or for his views on current matters to be passed on to the people concerned. Laski seldom sent just a brief formal note to his staff. However pressed, he invariably managed to comment on one or two topics of mutual interest. He was always meticulous in saying 'thank you' for services rendered and in inquiring about his staff's welfare and their personal activities. Ever anxious that they had adequate time off the job, if his cottage at Little Barnfield in Essex was likely to be unoccupied he would not hesitate to extend an invitation to his personal staff to make use of it during holidays. Mrs Derer recalled joining students, lecturers and visiting friends, often from abroad, at evenings in Laski's home in Fulham. There he held regular weekly 'at homes' which were more in the nature of seminars than 'coffee evenings'. One left quickly when they were over. Rather formal occasions, they were held in a completely book-lined study, the only space left on the walls being used for signed photographs of world statesmen.

I have often heard it said that Laski was so anxious to help his students that he sometimes gave them testimonials and letters of introduction that went at least a little beyond what was really justified by their qualities and relationship. He was also always willing to help in small and sometimes even large ways, people he did not himself know but who were recommended to him by friends and acquaintances. Mrs Derer told me of one such instance. She said:

A friend of my future husband came to this country from Czechoslovakia in 1949. We did not meet Laski on his visit but just before leaving London for home he asked me to ask Laski if he would autograph a book of his he had bought. Laski not only agreed but wrote 'To Comrade——— (putting in the man's name) with fraternal greetings'. When he got home, by some Freudian slip, the man left the inscribed book by mistake at the headquarters of the Czech

Communist Party where he had been paying a visit. It was soon found and he was interrogated for days as to his exact relationship with the 'Social Fascist' Laski. In view of the written evidence no one believed he had never even met Professor Laski and when he was arrested a few months later he was convinced it was due to this incident. In fact it turned out that the charges on which he was eventually convicted (and for which he served ten years) were entirely fictitious.

CHAPTER THREE

PEOPLE AND POLITICS

There were some who considered that Laski, a university professor, should not have played the very active part he did, for so many years, in day-to-day party politics. On this he made two points. His first one was that whilst, from time to time, there were protests about his support, as an academic, for the Labour Party (including his writing for the *Daily Herald*) and there was criticism of his efforts to encourage the adoption of more left-wing policies, no protests were ever heard about academics who wrote for 'capitalist' newspapers or supported other political parties, one of whom—which he gave as an example—was a member of the executive of the Liberal Party. Laski's second point was that in order to teach politics properly it was essential to have firsthand knowledge of politics. Classic textbooks had their full place, of course, he argued, but there was a great deal that could only be learned by practical experience in the cut and thrust world of day-to-day politics. To teach politics properly, he claimed, it was essential to have practice as well as theory.

Laski once said he gained more knowledge about the issues raised in administration from serving in local government than from reading textbooks. Living as he did in Fulham, he was elected an Alderman of the Council there in 1934 when Labour gained control and he served until 1945. As chairman of the Libraries Committee Laski took an especial pride in building up what has been described as one of the best public library services in London. He played a full part in general Council work and his advice was particularly sought when appointments were being made as he was considered to be a good judge of the qualities of applicants for posts being filled. It was in great part due to his zeal that housing redevelopment plans were drawn up resulting in a slum area being replaced by a modern council estate. Laski represented the Council on the Fulham Historical Society, the London District (Whitley) Council for Local Authorities and the Metropolitan Boroughs' Law and Planning Committee. His longest serving committee period—eight years—was as a member of the Borough's Law and Parliamentary Committee. During the closing days of 1974 a Greater London Council blue plaque was erected outside his Fulham house in Addison Bridge Place recording that he lived for the last twenty-four years of his life there.

As we have already seen, as soon as he took up his post at the London School of Economics, Laski spoke of it as an opportunity to 'bring real political influence within my grasp' and very shortly afterwards he was attending a week-end party arranged by Beatrice and Sidney Webb 'for Frida and me to meet the intelligentsia of the Labour movement'. The role he was mapping out for himself then—and which he strove to play for the remainder of his life—was that of *eminence grise* to those in the seats of political power.

Laski had several invitations to stand for Parliament, particularly during his early years at the London School of Economics. In November 1921 he told Holmes: 'I had a very hard job of refusing four different requests that I stand for Parliament at the next election. Hard because when a group of working men pay their own expenses to London to tell you they want you for the Member it is very difficult not to agree. But I weighed the agony of going to the House and finding myself in a hopeless minority against the possibility of doing a really big book on the theory of politics and I feel pretty certain that the latter is the more important. I don't know how long I shall feel that way.' In March 1923 he was writing: 'I have had a most tempting offer to stand for Parliament, a miners' seat where the majority is ten thousand and I have turned it down without a shadow of regret in order to go on with my book.' When Labour took office for the first time, in December 1923, Laski said that the new Prime Minister, Ramsay MacDonald, 'offered me a Cabinet post if I would fight an election and I found myself barely tempted, what a tribute to the attractiveness of learning'. And whilst I was writing this book an official of a Middlesex constituency Labour Party forty years ago sent me a copy of a letter he had had from Laski in 1930 declining an invitation to be adopted as prospective Parliamentary candidate.

When Ramsay MacDonald was forming his second Administration in 1929, Laski gave as his reasons for refusing the Prime Minister's offer of a seat in the House of Lords: 'I haven't the money; I want my independence; and I am a scholar by vocation and not a politician.' On several occasions Laski declared himself against the House of Lords. In the course of a talk given in 1941 on BBC radio under the title 'Why the House of Lords should be Abolished' he said:

> I am unable to believe, as the leaders of my Party believe, that a second chamber is a necessary instrument of wise government. Of course, I know that a second chamber is deeply rooted in the historical traditions of our Constitution but I agree with the great jurist who said that we need a better justification for some legal principle than it is many hundred years old. The test of an institution is whether it serves adequately a vital social need. On second chambers, I agree with the famous Frenchman, Sieyes, who remarked that when a second chamber agrees with the first it is superfluous, and that when it disagrees it is obnoxious. I do not think we begin to legislate in this country with reckless haste; on the contrary, far too often our action lags unpardonably behind the need it is intended to meet.

Laski always seized the opportunity to talk—privately if possible—with people in positions of influence and he liked to think that he was able to influence their thinking and shape events. In 1929, during the life of the second Labour Government, he told Holmes, 'the Lord Chancellor (Lord Sankey) came over for a night and we had a good talk. He's a fine fellow, high-minded without obtrusive moral principle and full of shrewd judgements. He has a judge to appoint in the autumn and we had a jolly time compiling the "points" for and against possible candidates. At least I spiked the guns of one fellow . . .'.

Commenting that two of his colleagues at the School had been given office in the new MacDonald Administration, he said: 'I was only able to elevate one from a very minor post to the Under-Secretaryship of Foreign Affairs (Hugh Dalton who held a Readership in Economics).' He added that he had had 'a long talk with the Prime Minister about America' and that Arthur Henderson, the Foreign Secretary, had asked for a memorandum.

Laski commented that 'the panting excitement of the aspirants to office made me grateful that I had not chosen a political career' and he spoke of 'sitting in the Prime Minister's room while he interviewed the hopefuls'.

However, Laski was bitterly disillusioned with the part played by Ramsay MacDonald in the 1931 financial crisis and their friendship ceased. As Prime Minister of the Labour Government he had, following disagreement in the Cabinet on measures to meet the desperately serious situation, gone to Buckingham Palace to tender his resignation. However, following a talk with the King and an appeal by His Majesty, he had returned to Downing Street to announce that he himself had been entrusted with the task of forming a temporary 'National' Government in which Baldwin and other Conservative Ministers as well as Liberals, agreed to serve under his leadership. In the October General Election which followed the crisis measures taken by the Government, Labour—led by Arthur Henderson—was completely routed, the number of their MPs falling from 289 to 46, and MacDonald continued as Prime Minister of a Conservative-dominated Administration.

Writing in the new year, Laski bitterly criticised MacDonald in a pamphlet, *The Crisis and the Constitution*, claiming that he had acted unconstitutionally, that 'crowned influence has rarely exercised so profound an influence in modern times' and that if MacDonald were to become at variance with the Conservatives 'we shall have either an ordinary Tory Cabinet or a manœuvring for position in which the real balance of power will turn upon the will of the King'. He told Holmes in one of his letters that he had been invited by the King's private secretary to discuss with him the position of the Crown in a constitutional crisis and said 'he picked my brains with skill'. On the subject of the monarchy, Laski, writing in a Socialist League pamphlet said:

> The most delicate of all problems confronted by a Socialist Government hinges upon the position of the monarchy. Its prestige and influence are enormous; its popularity is great; and any abandonment of the Crown of its assumed neutrality would precipitate a Constitutional crisis of which it would be impossible to overestimate the magnitude. No one can doubt that the existence of the monarchy makes the realisation of Socialism a peculiarly difficult adventure. ... This does not mean that Socialists ought forthwith to lay their

plans for a conflict with the monarchy which would end in the establishment of a republic. That would be a great misdirection of effort, even though a monarchy and a Socialist democracy are not, in the long run, easily compatible.

Laski told Holmes in October 1928 that he had had a 'sudden summons' to Downing Street to see the Conservative Prime Minister, Stanley Baldwin. He went on:

When I got in the PM's presence he said with extraordinary kindness that he had followed my work with great care and wanted to offer me the secretaryship of the research committee of the Cabinet with a salary about three times what I earn now. My breath was taken away and I said that I must have a day or two to think it over. After talking with Frida I went to see him this morning and declined it. For it would mean (1) that I could write no more; (2) that I should research into things I might not believe in; and (3) that my hands and tongue would be tied. He was extraordinarily kind and said he regretted it as much for his sake as any other, but Lord Haldane had urged it strongly and that he knew no one more fit for the post. Then he urged me to go in for politics and tried to explain to me that I had a big career there. I was very moved by his kindness but, of course, without a shred of doubt that what I am doing, especially with the independence it connotes, was five times more worth while than any official job. He could not have been more kind and I felt that, after all, the mere offer was some little justification of what I have been trying to do. But I'm quite sure I was right. It would be appalling to be silenced and not to be able to work with the people and the things I really care about. Liberty once felt is too precious to make it worth while to go into harness.

A London University inquiry was the outcome of a speech Laski made in Russia in 1934 and which was widely reported in the British Press. It also led to considerable newspaper correspondence and Questions in Parliament. It was reported that, in his Moscow speech, he had spoken of what was likely to happen if the Labour Party won an anticipated General Election. He suggested the advice that Ramsay MacDonald (then Prime Minister in a 'National' Government and despised by the Labour Party) would give to the King, and, after commenting that this would be a violation of the spirit of the British Constitution, he added: 'When the rules of the game prove unsuitable for victory the gentlemen of England change the rules of the game.' He was reported to have said that a Labour Premier 'must only take

People and Politics

office if he had obtained in advance the King's pledge to create enough Peers to swamp the Lords'.

Laski was also reported to have said that he anticipated a Conservative victory at the coming General Election (here his forecast proved correct), and that the crisis would deepen, and the Conservatives would be forced to go in for strong government, suspending various liberties and probably repealing the Habeas Corpus Act. The actual suspension—or suppression—of the Constitution would follow. Decaying capitalism would meet wider and wider resistance from the working class, there would be strikes everywhere and worse than that in the 'distressed areas', the Clyde, parts of the North, and South Wales, involving immediate suspension of the Parliamentary system. Laski said he did not think that there would develop in England (except in the event of a disastrous war) the temper of successful revolution until a Labour Government had attempted to govern by Act of Parliament.

In the House of Commons the Financial Secretary to the Treasury, Duff Cooper, was asked whether his attention had been called to a lecture on the prospects of revolution in Great Britain delivered in Russia by Professor Harold Laski, of the London School of Economics, and whether, in view of the fact that the School was supported by a grant from His Majesty's Government, he would take steps to indicate that the said grant was not given with the object of facilitating activities of that kind. Duff Cooper, in reply, said he had seen the reports in the Press, and the London School of Economics did not receive a grant directly from the Government. The University of London received an annual block grant, paid on the advice of the University Grants Committee and from this source and others at its disposal made allocations to its various constituent schools and colleges. He added that it did not seem to him to be necessary to take any action of the nature suggested by the questioner.

After the questioner had then jumped up to ask if 'Professor Laski is an avowed Communist as well as being of alien origin', Sir Stafford Cripps, from the Opposition front bench, commented: 'Is the Right Hon. Gentleman aware that the charter of the London School of Economics expressly provides for complete freedom for professors and lecturers to express their political opinions outside the School and will he resist the obvious tendency to try to curtail that freedom?' The matter was allowed to drop after a Labour Member, James Maxton, had commented that Laski was 'a perfectly respectable member of the Party which composes His Majesty's Official Opposition' but the following day a Question was addressed to the Foreign Secretary about Laski being granted permission to visit the USSR. Sir John Simon replied that no special facilities were required for visits to the Soviet Union.

This was soon followed by a statement by the Vice-Chancellor and Principal of the University of London saying that Laski's action would form the subject of inquiry and that 'the University accepts no responsibility for personal expressions of opinion by any of its professors'. Then came a letter to *The Times* signed by five members of the teaching staff at the School (R. S. T. Chorley, T. A. Gregory, Eileen Power, R. H. Tawney and Charles K. Webster) expressing the view that 'in our judgement a university teacher is entitled to express his opinion with the same freedom and with the same limits as any other British citizen. Any other course would be, in our view, a grave dereliction of duty. The novel suggestion that a university may properly conduct an inquiry into expressions of opinion by its teachers on matters of public interest appears to us a menace to academic freedom and to national well-being'.

A few days after the Questions in Parliament the Emergency Committee of the School passed a resolution giving it as their view 'that the development of public opinion concerning Professor Laski's recent more popular utterances is, in fact, rightly or wrongly, against the best interests of the School and ought now to be taken by him into account in deciding on "personal duty" under the Professorial Council Resolution of 1931'. The 1931 resolution referred to laid down a provision about outside paid work by full-time teachers other than examining for the School or University and occasional writing and the giving of one or two special lectures. Laski replied: 'I regard myself as free to make occasional speeches on political topics, especially at such times as a General Election. I also regard myself as bound, in making such speeches, by the general sense of the resolution passed by the Professorial Council in 1931'.

The Professorial Council (precursor of the Academic Board) and the Court of Governors had resolved that 'while members of the staff ... should ... be free from regulation or censure by the

Governors of the School in respect of their writings or public speeches, they should regard it as a personal duty to preserve in such writings or speeches a proper regard for the reputation of the School as an academic centre of scientific research'. Maynard Keynes wrote to the *New Statesman* inquiring if it was usual for the University of London to express opinions on the views of its professors. 'What', he asked, 'is the appropriate body for this purpose? One had assumed it to be well established in England, as distinguished from Moscow or Berlin, that a professor is entitled to the unfettered expression of his opinions and that no one but himself has any responsibility in the matter. What are we coming to? Fortunately the Founders of the London School of Economics with a wise foresight, expressly provided in its Charter for the complete freedom of its teachers in the expression of their political opinions.'

Laski's only public comment on the affair was that his Moscow remarks had been misquoted and taken from their context, adding: 'I believe it to be a genuine case of a reporter misunderstanding that these remarks were intended as a summary of the Communist case and not my own views.'

The articles which Laski wrote for newspapers (and especially those for the *Daily Herald*) were the subject of a serious clash with the School's Director, Sir William Beveridge, who took exception to one of his staff being associated with such popular journalism. Amongst the articles which Laski had for many years contributed to the *Herald* were a considerable number of sketches of contemporary figures. They included such personalities as Arthur Henderson, George Lansbury, Dean Inge, Oswald Mosley, Winston Churchill, Lord Birkenhead, Bertrand Russell, R. H. Tawney, Bernard Shaw, H. G. Wells, Rudyard Kipling, John Galsworthy, Lord Beaverbrook and Sir Austen Chamberlain. Laski claimed that he had the right under the conditions of his appointment to undertake any work he chose—providing of course that he was not neglecting his School duties—but Beveridge told him that he ought to consult the School Governors about his journalist activities.

This Laski did, writing to Sir Arthur Steel-Maitland, the Chairman. In the course of his letter he set out his responsibilities at the School, showing just how many hours each term he devoted to lecturing, supervising and giving help and advice to a host of students. He claimed that having fulfilled his School duties (and no one could challenge the wholehearted way he met his responsibilities, never sparing himself either during School hours or at week-ends) he had a clear right to add to his income by freelance journalism. He emphasised that he was a teacher by vocation and that during the time the articles had appeared his reputation had not in any way suffered, he having accepted invitations to lecture at other English universities, on the continent of Europe and in the United States. He had turned down invitations from India and China. However, Laski offered to discontinue the articles if that was the wish of the Governors and the outcome was that he eventually did, but under protest.

Along with others associated with the School, Laski, after the initial period when things had gone very smoothly, had not for some time found it easy to work with Sir William Beveridge who had only become Director in 1919 just a few months before Laski joined the staff. As a young man Beveridge had been sub-warden of Toynbee Hall in the East End of London and an occasional student at the School from 1903 to 1905. Later a leader writer on the *Morning Post*, he subsequently joined the Civil Service to organise the Employment Exchanges, and during the 1914–18 war, after working in the Ministry of Munitions, was later appointed permanent secretary to the Ministry of Food. It was from there that Beveridge went to the School and he was soon joined by Mrs Janet Mair, as School secretary. She had worked with him closely in the Civil Service and they were married following the death of her husband who was Beveridge's cousin.

The period following Beveridge's appointment as Director had been a time of extensive development, rapid change and very substantial increase in the numbers of students. All this had necessitated a considerably enlarged teaching staff and Laski had not been alone in feeling that Beveridge was altogether too autocratic. He himself had seemed unaware of the feelings of the members of the staff towards him, saying later: 'I never had power in an absolute sense. I worked persistently to make such power as I had a thing to be exercised only in consultation with my colleagues'. However, one of the School's professors commented at the time 'dictators always consult somebody but what we are here to establish is not consultation by choice but consultation by rule'.

As time went on Beveridge had set up a number of committees

which had the effect of strengthening his position. One was an Emergency Committee of the Governors which, as he admitted, 'once established became in practice the governing body of the School'. R. S. T. Chorley (now Lord Chorley) for many years Professor of Commercial and Industrial Law at the School, has commented that with this committee in his pocket, but only so long as it was so, Beveridge could always trump the Professorial Council, and so long as it continued to do what he wanted his 'benevolent autocracy' was a reality. After a few years, however, the Emergency Committee's constitution was amended to include members of the Professorial Council (one of whom was Laski) and this, with other emendations, contributed towards democratisation of the School.

Until some members of the School teaching staff became associated with the Labour movement (including Clement Attlee, Hugh Dalton and H. B. Lees-Smith) Beveridge had had no objection to combining university teaching with politics, indeed, during his discussions with Sidney Webb about becoming Director he had asked if there would be objection to his agreeing to stand for Parliament if invited. Later, however, he made known his view that 'combining a political career with an academic career in the social sciences' was all wrong and advised against it. It was a considerable source of irritation to him that his view was not heeded.

Laski was amongst those who did not accept Beveridge's advice, claiming that he was playing the game within the rules and stressing that he had no intention of entering Parliament. Lord Chorley (with whom I had a most helpful talk about Laski's association with the School) told me that one day when some observations of Laski's were being widely quoted in the national newspapers, he met him coming from the Director's room. 'Seeing him looking somewhat rueful', Lord Chorley told me, 'I asked Laski what had been happening and he replied, "I have just been getting a wigging from the Director. He says I am a liability to the School and not an asset!"'

All this did not help the already strained relationship between Laski and the Director, and when Beveridge resigned in 1937 to become Master of University College, Oxford, Laski was greatly relieved. He warmly welcomed the appointment of Sir Alexander Carr-Saunders, telling his friends that it had made a world of difference to his life. It was a friendship that was to deepen as time went on, and Laski said that, to him, the School, under Carr-Saunders, had become 'an idyll'.

In 1930, during the period of the second Labour Government Laski was so concerned at attacks being made on Stanley Baldwin, the Leader of the Conservatives, by his own Party that he felt obliged to write him a letter. Lord Rothermere's newspapers (including the *Daily Mail*) had for some time been criticising his leadership and so Baldwin called a special meeting of Conservative MPs, peers and candidates and in the course of his speech he linked Lord Beaverbrook (of the *Daily Express*) and Lord Rothermere with William Randolph Hearst, the American press tycoon, saying 'there is nothing more curious in modern evolution than the effect of an enormous fortune rapidly made and the control of newspapers of your own'. Baldwin went on to produce a letter Lord Rothermere had written in which he said he would not support Baldwin unless he had complete guarantees as to policy 'and unless I am acquainted with the names of at least eight or ten of his most prominent colleagues in the next Ministry'. Baldwin told his audience: 'These are the terms that your leader would have to accept and when sent for by the King he would have to say "Sire, these names are not necessarily my choice but they have the support of Lord Rothermere". A more preposterous and insolent demand was never made on the leader of any political party. I repudiate it with contempt and I will fight that attempt at domination to the end.' In the course of his letter to Baldwin, Laski wrote: 'There are many socialists who, like myself... feel grateful for the quality of human directness you bring to our political life.... We resent, not less than your own friends, the effort to usurp a leadership the distinction of which has been, if I may say so, an honoured feature of our time.'

Not long before the 1932 annual conference of the Labour Party there were developments within the movement that resulted in Laski becoming an influential member of a newly-formed body calling itself the Socialist League. There were two events that led up to its creation. A number of prominent members of the Party had had meetings—at Easton Lodge in Essex at the invitation of the Countess of Warwick—to consider the reasons for Labour's defeat at the previous General Election, and they had agreed upon the course to be pursued to try and persuade the annual Party conference to adopt a more aggressive policy 'as an alternative to gradualism'.

Very shortly afterwards there arose a serious split in the ranks of the Independent Labour Party (which had been one of the pioneer organisations in the formation of the Labour Party) and when a decision was taken to disaffiliate from the Labour Party some ILP members who had decided to remain loyal to the Labour Party joined a number of those who had met at Easton Lodge to form the Socialist League. Laski was elected a member of the executive committee of the new body which also included Sir Stafford Cripps, Sir Charles Trevelyan, William Mellor (ex-editor of the *Daily Herald*), G. D. H. Cole, R. H. Tawney, C. R. Attlee (then deputy leader of the Parliamentary Labour Party), Aneurin Bevan, Ellen Wilkinson and D. N. Pritt. A programme was devised which it was considered the next Labour Government should carry out and which included legislation 'to forestall sabotage by financial interests'; abolition of the House of Lords; nationalisation of banks, land, mines, power, transport, cotton and iron and steel; and the acceptance of the principle of work or maintenance. For the next few years—with Laski playing a full part—the members of the Socialist League put forward proposals, in various forms, to the annual conferences of the Labour Party and they were defeated on every occasion.

In 1937 there was another development which brought Laski to the fore. In that year the Independent Labour Party, the Communist Party and the Socialist League published a jointly-signed 'Unity Manifesto', urging 'unity in the struggle against Fascism, reaction and war' and against the 'National' Government led by Neville Chamberlain. Its objects, which most readily appealed to Laski, included such phrases as 'the adoption of a fighting programme of mass struggle, through the democratisation of the Labour Party and the trade union movement'. It rejected what it called 'class collaboration' and recorded its 'implacable opposition to the rearmament and recruiting programme of the Government'. The Manifesto, which was signed by, in addition to Laski, such well-known political figures as Aneurin Bevan, Harry Pollitt, John Strachey, Palme Dutt and Sir Stafford Cripps, summoned the workers to 'mobilise for the maintenance of peace, for the defence of the Soviet Union and its fight for peace, and for a pact between Great Britain, the Soviet Union, France and all other states in which the working class have political freedom'. And the workers were urged to 'wage incessant struggle, political and industrial alike, for simple things the workers need'.

The Labour Party executive reacted to the 'Unity Manifesto' by declaring that united action with the Communist Party was incompatible with Labour Party membership and any organisation formed to pursue 'United Front' activities should not be given support by the Party. Moves to circumvent the ban led to a debate at the following annual conference of the Labour Party when Sir Stafford Cripps, in moving the reference back to that part of the national executive's report which condemned the unity campaign, said the ban imposed on association with the Communist Party and the ILP was 'not extended to those who associated themselves with members of opposing capitalist parties' a reference to such bodies as the National Peace Council. Laski was soon at the rostrum to support Cripps, declaring that if he had to choose between appearing on the same platform with Winston Churchill or Harry Pollitt (the Communist leader) he had no doubt at all that his proper place was with Pollitt. After a long debate the reference back of the executive's report was heavily defeated on both the issues of the Socialist League (membership of which had been declared incompatible with membership of the Labour Party) and the United Front, and the Party's official opposition to the Unity Manifesto was endorsed.

Laski's support for the officially condemned Unity campaign and Socialist League had done nothing to weaken his popularity with Labour Party conference delegates. At that same 1937 annual conference changes were made in the Party constitution which gave local constituency Labour Parties the right to elect a number of their own nominees to the national executive, and Laski was given a seat which he retained until—by his own choice—he retired from the executive in 1949.

The slogan 'Popular Front' (by way of reference to the French *Front Populaire* and the Spanish *Frente Popular*) was in vogue in 1937 and whilst both movements on the continent rested on a broader base than that of the working class—including radicals as well as socialists—the demand in Britain had been principally one for joint action between the Labour Party and the Communists. This development was opposed by the Labour Party executive and although Laski understood the objects of the movement which he regarded as serving a limited purpose, that of mobilising public opinion against the foreign policy of the Chamberlain Government, he was always opposed to any permanent alliance with the Communists. When, therefore, in May 1938, the Labour Party executive decided to issue a statement under the title *Labour and the Popular Front* Laski wrote the pamphlet which was a devastating indictment of the Communist technique. Morgan Phillips, then Labour Party secretary, kept the manuscript, in Laski's handwriting, and quoted from it on at least one public occasion the phrase that the Communist 'policy is devoid of any certainty. They are committed rather to manœuvre than to principle. They would be capable of stabbing us in the back at any time or involving us in joint responsibility for their political indiscretions'.

It is an interesting and closely reasoned document written in typical Laski style. It starts off by referring to the profound apprehension about international relationships and the foreign policy of the Government which had led

a number of people, including some of our friends, to consider the possibility of a new political combination which, they urge, should be formed to bring down the Chamberlain Government and substitute a new and wiser administration in its place. What is known as the 'Popular Front' or 'Democratic Peace Alliance' is, so say its advocates, the high-road to immediate victory.

And then he goes on to analyse the argument that in so grave an international situation the Labour Party should temporarily abandon its traditional policy of political independence and its socialist principles. On the right of the Labour Party there would be the Liberals and such Conservatives both inside and outside Parliament as would lend their support. On its left, the Communist Party and the Independent Labour Party. The pamphlet says it is not believed that the proposed combination would afford a better rallying cry than the Labour Party itself. The Liberals are referred to as 'a diminishing force' and uncertainty is expressed as to what the attitude of Liberal voters would be whilst 'we ourselves should regard Communist participation as an electoral liability rather than an asset. The Communist Party is subject to political directions from abroad and to this extent is not allowed to determine its own policy. Both the Labour Party and the Liberals would be distracted from the main purpose of the proposed combination by the need to protect themselves against Communist manœuvres. The presence of the Communists would bring some few thousand votes to the alliance but it might well drive millions into Mr Chamberlain's camp'.

And so Laski's pamphlet goes on, with an expression of the belief:

> that there is an increasing probability of a Labour victory at the next election and that such a victory would be hindered by the building of an artificial combination, ineffective and embarrassing to its partners and unlikely to impress the bulk of the electorate.

And Laski concluded the pamphlet by saying:

> Do not let us compromise our socialist convictions. Let us, rather, work with renewed energy for the triumph of the ideals we have inherited. Never has it been so clear as now that their achievement is the condition of democracy and peace. Never was it so urgent as now to serve those ideals with high courage and with iron determination.

Later, in 1938, of course, there was the Czech crisis and the Munich settlement. The international situation was indeed grim when, at the 1939 Labour Party conference, Sir Stafford Cripps appealed unsuccessfully against expulsion for pursuing the Popular Front idea. In a couple of months Britain was at war.

The years that followed did nothing to change Laski's opinion of the Communists, and in 1946 he wrote—and signed—a pamphlet for the Labour Party entitled *The Secret Battalion* in which he said of the Communists 'they act like a secret battalion of paratroopers within the brigade whose discipline they have accepted. They meet secretly to propose their own line of action; they have one set of rules to regulate their conduct one to another, and a different set of rules to be observed towards those who are not in the battalion'.

It is a 32-page pamphlet in which, referring to the

> real purpose inherent in the strategy which Communists are ultimately determined to employ, [he says] it assumes the inevitability of violent revolution; therefore it infers that democracy in the British form, with its reliance on constitutional methods, is no more than a temporary phase between the forcible seizure of power by the bour-

geoisie and the forcible seizure of power by the proletariat. Since it regards itself as the vanguard of the proletariat, the Communist Party must permeate the ranks of the Labour Party in order to dominate its life. Thus only can it prepare for that dictatorship which is the necessary method of consolidating its authority after the proletariat has hurled the bourgeoisie from power. It therefore works, quite deliberately, towards the one-party state. It denies the right of opposition, the rule of law, freedom of speech or association, the duty of the individual citizen to put his own conscience before the party's orders.

Laski was always ready to comment on affairs of the day and wide publicity was generally given to what he had to say. During the 1930s there was considerable criticism of the BBC, and its Director-General, Sir John Reith, was under regular attack on a number of fronts, one of which was the contents of the Sunday radio programmes. Laski on that occasion joined in the chorus of criticism with:

Sunday is what the lawyers call a *dies non* on the wireless because Sir John thinks that Bloomsbury is good for us. To him, doubtless, we also owe the flawless Oxford accents of the announcers.... He speaks with the urgency of a pontiff.... You too rarely hear from the admirable staff he has gathered about him. He gives the impression that the BBC pivots too exclusively upon his private sense of right and wrong. We have endless sermons from St Martin-in-the-Fields, could not Sir John risk a communist? Can we have a discussion on birth control? Can we not hear about the Five Year Plan? I am agreeing that Sir John is a big man. But no man is ever big enough to exercise what is practically unlimited power. He must learn that the wicked heresies of today are the sober commonplaces of tomorrow.

At the time of the constitutional crisis created in 1936 by King Edward VIII's desire to marry Wallis Simpson, a twice-divorced American lady, Laski came out strongly on the side of Prime Minister Stanley Baldwin and the Cabinet. In a signed newspaper article on 'Crown and Cabinet' he stressed the salient fact that under the British constitution the Cabinet and not the King was politically supreme. In those circumstances, the King had no alternative but to accept the Cabinet's 'advice' in all matters, they being responsible for his acts. Laski said that royal opposition to the established Government, if carried to its logical conclusion, could only end in one of two things—monarchical dictatorship or abdication.

As we have seen, Laski did a great deal of travelling around the country. Not surprisingly he had all kinds of experiences and on a number of occasions his American friend Holmes begged him to be assured that he enjoyed the variety in his letters. This encouraged Laski to sometimes refer to happenings far removed from the world of politics and learning. In one of his letters Laski told Holmes that he had been to Manchester for a few days and:

> I stepped from the train and at the barrier found a policeman's hand descend heavily upon my shoulder. 'Well, Toscini, we have been expecting you,—come quietly.' I never refuse an invitation that has the prospect of interest so I walked quietly and silently to the police-station. I was then charged as Luigi Toscini with being concerned in an Italian jewel-shop robbery in Manchester on the 6th August and was asked if I had anything to say. I said 'yes' and explained who I was. After a minute or two my accent must have been revealing as the entire police force of Manchester seemed to arrive and apologise. I then had a whiskey with the inspector and spent the next three days in receiving grinning salutes from policemen on the streets. You will admit that it was a distinguished arrival. I admit that, on the evidence of photographs, it was a perfectly reasonable mistake. The police were so relieved that I made no fuss that I do not believe I could now be arrested in Manchester.

Laski, not surprisingly, was deeply concerned during the 1930s at the plight of the unemployed, and when in January 1933 the number registered as out of work reached the record figure of 2,955,000 he commented that the official statistics did not tell the full story. 'I estimate', he said, 'there is in addition a substantial number of unregistered workless which would bring the total to over three and a half million.'

The marches to London of unemployed men and women from the North-East, Scotland, South Wales and other 'Depressed Areas' during those years are now part of social history. There were, of course, very many workless in southern England (the figures for Middlesex were just over 4 per cent) but nothing like that of some parts of the country where up to a third of the working population were 'on the dole'. In one of his speeches Laski said: 'In going round the country I've met many men who have grown from boyhood to manhood and have never had the chance of a day's work.' The marchers' objectives were to lobby MPs, to hold mass meetings, and to draw the attention of the nation to their desperate plight. Very many had been out of work for years and had given up hope.

Of course, the health of the workless and their families suffered and this was one of the aspects about which Laski expressed particular concern. He used to quote Sir George Newman, Chief Medical Officer of Health for England and Wales, who said in his 1933 Report 'no fewer than two million homes were stricken by death or disease. There was distress, privation, physical and mental, in areas severely depressed by unemployment' and a year later Newman wrote: 'The State which allows its own people to degenerate physically and mentally because of unemployment is incurring a grave responsibility for the future. Have the Authorities failed to recognise this?'

Laski repeatedly condemned the Government for their indifference to the unemployed and for the way in which they were degraded and humiliated by the family Means Test and the Poor Law, and he protested, too, at the attitude of the authorities to the men and women who, from time to time, tramped their way to London. They were generally well received by the people in the towns and villages they passed through on their way, being fed and accommodated as comfortably as possible in schools and public halls. When early in 1934 one of the marches took place Laski supported those who felt that the authorities went out of their way to create an apprehensive atmosphere in the capital. Sir John Gilmour, the Home Secretary, warned the public to be cautious and careful. Shopkeepers were urged to put up their shutters in case of 'possible bloodshed' and warnings were given to children in the London schools.

Not without reason, there were fears of *agent provocateurs* being planted to stir up trouble (there were those who were convinced this had happened on previous occasions) and even suggestions that the police would ban the tired and leg-weary men and women from entering London. It was in this atmosphere that Laski played a prominent part in the setting up of a committee of prominent people to watch and study the conduct of the Metropolitan police and to come to the defence of the marchers if acts of provocation were committed. As the marchers neared London the *Manchester Guardian* published the following letter:

The present hunger march has been preceded by public statements by the Home Secretary and the Attorney-General (who has already hinted at the possibility of bloodshed) which we feel justify apprehension. Furthermore, certain features of the police preparations for the present march—for example, instructions to shopkeepers to barricade their windows—cannot but create an atmosphere of misgiving, not only dangerous but unjustified by the facts.

All reports bear witness to the excellent discipline of the marchers. From their own leaders they have received repeated instructions of the strictest character, warning them against any breach of the peace, even under extreme provocation.

In view of the general and alarming tendency to encroachment on the liberty of the citizen, there has recently been formed a Council of Civil Liberties. One of the special duties of this Council will be to maintain a vigilant observation of the proceedings of the next few days. Relevant and well-authenticated reports by responsible people will be welcomed and investigated by the Council.

(Signed)

Lascelles Abercrombie	C. R. Attlee
Ambrose Appelbe	V. R. Brittain
Dudley Collard	A. P. Herbert
Harold Laski	D. N. Pritt
G. H. Bing	Kingsley Martin
Evelyn Sharp Nevinson	H. G. Wells
Henry W. Nevinson	Ronald Kidd
Edith Summerskill	(Secretary)

As one would expect, the authorities, knowing about the activities of the committee, were restrained in their attitude and there were, of course, no disturbances. Laski was one who spent a considerable time outside the Houses of Parliament, in Hyde Park and elsewhere attending the rallies and demonstrations with a watchful eye and, as one London evening newspaper put it: 'The marchers have shamed their detractors by their dignity and surprised those who know their grievances best by their restraint.' It is interesting to note that the National Council of Civil Liberties of today was established as a direct outcome of this occasion.

Laski was one of those present in the public gallery of the House of Commons to listen to a debate following the House's rejection of an appeal that a deputation from the marchers be heard at the Bar of the House. The following day one London newspaper reported, under the heading 'House Packed at Midnight Drama':

The Prime Minister's refusal to allow the hunger marchers to voice their grievance, either to himself, the Cabinet, or the House, was criticised in a crowded House of Commons last night. Every seat was occupied and MPs stood in a dense throng beyond the Bar to hear the case for the marchers. MacDonald sat on the front Government bench supported by all the prominent Members of the Cabinet. It was an unusual spectacle, this indictment of a Prime Minister by MPs who spoke on behalf of unemployed men who had tramped from all parts of the country to put their grievances before Parliament.

Two years later, in 1936, Laski was amongst those who welcomed to London two hundred unemployed men who had tramped from the stricken town of Jarrow to present a petition to the then Prime Minister, Stanley Baldwin. They were led by the town's MP, Ellen Wilkinson, for whom Laski had a great admiration and with whom he was closely associated politically for many years. And when it was all over the marchers left King's Cross station by special train and were given a great reception when they arrived home. Not surprisingly, Laski was amongst those who were appalled at the attitude of the local Unemployment Assistance Board who immediately deducted a few shillings from the marchers' scanty allowances because, it was claimed, they had absented themselves from Jarrow and were not available for work had any turned up. And most of them had been unemployed for years!

Early in 1936 publisher Victor Gollancz and John Strachey, once described as the most articulate Marxist spokesman of his day, decided to launch what they chose to call the Left Book Club. Aiming to build a United Front against Fascism and to organise public opinion to that end, it was an immediate success, it soon becoming clear there was a demand throughout the country for books about left-wing political subjects. By the end of May the Club had a membership of over 12,000 regular subscribers who guaranteed to purchase monthly book choices on publication at a price of 2s. 6d. a volume. By the spring of 1939 the membership figure was 60,000 although it never reached the 100,000 mark hoped for at the outset by Gollancz. Many subscribers (it attracted members from all classes of society) were registered with their local booksellers whilst others chose to have their volumes regularly sent through the post. In areas where unemployment was particularly heavy, out-of-work men and women devised schemes of group membership, jointly contributing to the cost of the books and reading them in turn.

Gollancz and Strachey had very early on in their planning of the project told Laski what they had in mind. They found him most enthusiastic about the whole idea—it was something after his own heart—and he readily agreed to accept an invitation to join them on the selection committee. Henceforth he did all he could to make the venture a success. Bound from the outset in a very distinctive limp orange cloth, the volumes soon became a familiar sight on the bookshelves of the Left. On the outside of the cover were the words 'Left Book Club Edition—Not for Sale to the Public'.

In a Foreword to one of the monthly choices not long after the scheme started Gollancz wrote:

... While the three selectors of the Left Book Club choices—Strachey, Laski and myself—were all agreed that a Foreword was desirable, I alone am responsible for what is written here—though I think that Laski and Strachey would agree with me.

Why did we think that a Foreword was desirable? Because we find that many members—a surprisingly large number—have the idea that in some sort of way a Left Book Club Choice, first, represents the views of the three selectors, and secondly incorporates the Left Book Club 'policy'. A moment's thought should show that the first suggestion could be true only in the worst kind of Fascist State, and that the second is a contradiction in terms: but we get letters so frequently—most interesting and vital letters—which say 'surely you and Laski and Strachey cannot believe what So-and-So says on page so-and-so of Such-and-Such a book' that there can be no doubt at all that the misconception exists.

The plain facts are, of course (a) that the three selectors, although they have that broad general agreement without which successful committee work is impossible, differ as to shade and *nuance* of opinion in a hundred ways; (b) that even if they were in perfect agreement on every point, nothing could be worse than a stream of books which expressed the same point of view over and over again; and (c) that their only criterion for a Choice is whether or not the reading and discussion of it will be helpful for the general struggle against Fascism and war. And that brings me on to this question of Left Book Club 'policy'. The Left Book Club has no 'policy': or rather it has no policy other than that of equipping people to fight against war and Fascism. As I have said elsewhere, it would not even be true to say that the People's Front is the 'policy' of the Left Book Club, though all three selectors are enthusiastically in favour of it. What we rather feel is that by giving a wide distribution to books which represent many shades of Left opinion (and perhaps, most of all, by providing facilities for the discussion of those books in the 300 local centres and circles that have sprung up all over the country) we are creating the mass basis without which a genuine People's Front is impossible. In other words, the People's Front is not the 'policy' of the Left Book Club, but the very existence of the Left Book Club tends towards a People's Front.

Each monthly choice of book was accompanied by a copy of a journal called *Left Book News* (soon to be changed to *Left News*) which explained the aims of the Club, gave news about forthcoming publications, introduced the authors, and discussed the current selection. In an early editorial in the magazine Gollancz wrote: 'We have not the smallest doubt that the Left Book Club has struck just the right note to which a vast public up and down the country was waiting to respond. There must be no delay, brethren, no people who just read the books and the *News* and leave it at that. Every member must actively help by enlisting his friends, relations or associates.'

As time went on interest in the country was such that many local discussion groups were formed and met regularly. Some of them were set up on a professional basis; they included civil servants, lawyers, school-teachers, doctors and poets, the latter publishing an anthology of left-wing poetry. Interest was such that in 1937 the Club held a national Rally in London's Royal Albert Hall, the speakers including Sir Richard Acland, Sir Stafford Cripps, D. N. Pritt and Harry Pollitt. Special trains for the occasion were run from the Provinces at greatly reduced fares, the cost of the journey from Manchester, for example, being 10s.

One of the Club's first publications was *France Today and the People's Front* by a French communist, Maurice Thorez. Leonard Woolf contributed *Barbarians at the Gate*, W. H. Thomson *Civil Liberties* and Arthur Koestler *Spanish Testament*. Most of the books published by the Club over the years are little known today but amongst those that have achieved a permanent place is George Orwell's *The Road to Wigan Pier* which appeared in 1937. Other authors included Emile Burns, J. R. Campbell, G. D. H. Cole, Sir Stafford Cripps, Palme Dutt and Philip Noel-

Baker. Clement Attlee contributed his *The Labour Party in Perspective* and I have seen it stated that local discussion group leaders were given guidance to contrast it unfavourably with appropriate Marxist themes. Ellen Wilkinson's tragic story of the plight of the north-east town of Jarrow, with its army of unemployed men and women was a most popular choice. Under the title of *The Town That Was Murdered* it was told with a realism that helped to draw the nation's attention to the realities of the effects of mass unemployment.

As one would expect, Gollancz and Strachey also wrote books specially for the series, as did Laski, who very frequently contributed major book reviews to the *Left News*. Some books which had originally appeared in 1936 when the Club was formed were re-issued as monthly choices and amongst these was Strachey's *The Coming Struggle for Power*. The Club also published a considerable number of 'extra' choices in addition to each month's selection, and, amongst other activities, which Laski encouraged, there were competitions (with prizes) for a novel and for a book on unemployment.

It will be seen that Laski's appetite for work was, at this time, an insatiable as ever, and—in addition to his other regular commitments—he served for a time on the board of *Tribune*, the left-wing periodical founded by Sir Stafford Cripps and taken over by Gollancz in 1938. As one would expect, from then on considerable space was regularly devoted in the journal to the activities of the Left Book Club.

The non-aggression pact between Nazi Germany and the Soviet Union in the summer of 1939 was a big blow to those who had been using the Club from its inception as a vehicle for Communist propaganda. A very early edition of the *Left News* had contained a full draft of the Constitution of the USSR and there were frequent articles putting the Marxist viewpoint. There were those who all along felt that one of the main objects of the Club, to rally the forces against Fascism, was in danger of being lost sight of in the anxiety of some people to use it to further the Communist line.

Shortly after the outbreak of war in September 1939 Gollancz, Strachey and Laski were joint authors of a special *Left News* article reminding their readers that the aims of the Club were to assist in the fight against Fascism and to struggle for peace and 'a better social and economic order'. 'For us', they wrote, 'Hitler is a symptom of a deeper disease; he is not the disease itself.' Members of the Club were reminded that they must never cease to stress that 'we are fighting for a new world'. Laski was particularly anxious that readers of *Left News* should not be in any doubt as to where he stood following the pact between Hitler and Stalin, and he urged that 'socialists must work and hope for a British victory'.

The Left Book Club continued throughout the war with diminishing popularity, and after the 1945 General Election and Labour's victory, membership fell off rapidly, and—with nearly 250 books to its credit—the Club's activities eventually ceased. Laski maintained his interest in it to the end.

I have told earlier of Laski's readiness to assist his students at the London School of Economics in their careers and this help he extended to those in the political field. When George Brown (now Lord George-Brown), a very young area official of the Transport and General Workers' Union, was eager to have a chance to enter Parliament it was Laski who extended a friendly hand. He had been very favourably impressed with a speech Brown had made at the 1939 annual conference of the Labour Party and proposed that Brown should become Labour candidate for Dundee along with John Strachey (there were two-member constituencies in those days). However, when nothing came of that, Laski suggested that Brown should seek to be adopted for the Derbyshire constituency of Belper and did what he could to help. 'This was just what I wanted' he told me and, in spite of opposition from Ernest Bevin, then General Secretary of the Transport and General Workers' Union, Brown was sponsored by his union and, in due course, adopted. It is a matter of history now how he became Belper's MP, held the seat for twenty-five years and achieved high office in subsequent Labour Governments including those of Deputy Prime Minister and Foreign Secretary.

As a member of the Industrial Court for fifteen years, Laski gained a reputation for fairness and for the painstaking way in which he applied himself to the cases. Questions of awards in disputes between the Treasury and the Civil Service were often considerably involved and although he was nominally a representative of the staff side he maintained the confidence of all concerned. Independent chairman throughout the whole period Laski served, Sir Harold Morris, KC, described him as an 'ideal colleague'. As one would expect, he revelled in trying to sort out complicated situations and here again, as in so many other spheres, he was ever eager to apply himself to the drafting of formulae. He was anxious to ensure that people were adequately paid for their work but many of those with whom I have talked have commented that Laski himself cared little about money. It was quite common for him to stuff cheques in his pocket and forget to bank them. I have already referred to a number of instances where he readily opened his wallet and helped students who were in need of financial assistance. Those are only just a few of the examples that have come to light and there is good reason to believe that there were very many more. I have seen a letter which Morgan Phillips wrote to Laski, thanking him for a cheque for £50 which he had received 'on account' for royalties for one of his books and which he had asked should be paid into the Labour Party funds. Walter Citrine (now Lord Citrine) came into contact with Laski from time to time when he was General Secretary of the Trades Union Congress and he told me that Laski was not only always willing to do all he could to help with advice or service but 'he was ever ready to sit down and write an article at short notice without any thought whatever of financial reward'. As early as 1921 he was sending the royalties on one of his books 'to Vienna for the relief of destitute professors'. That same year when he received £70 on account for royalties he said: 'I looked round for the right object. I found a student who was the sole support of a mother and young sister who was killing himself to get a degree and keep them alive at the same time. Result, of course pneumonia. So I financed them in the convalescence, sent him away for ten days, put him in for his exam and found he'd got a brilliant first.'

At the height of World War II, in February 1942, Wing Commander James MP, expressed his regret in the House of Commons that Laski should be used by the British Broadcasting Corporation as a broadcaster 'when he went to America to evade military service during the 1914–18 war'. A few days later a letter from Laski appeared in the then *Manchester Guardian* refuting the charges. In the course of his letter, Laski said:

I volunteered for military service on August 5th, 1914, and was rejected on medical grounds. At the suggestion of my late tutor, Mr

Herbert Fisher, I then accepted a year's appointment at McGill University. On September 9th, 1915, I sought to enlist in the Canadian Army and was again rejected. In 1916 I was offered and accepted a post in Harvard University. In July 1917, I again sought to enlist in the British army at British Recruiting Office in New York and was again refused on medical grounds. I may add that I hold a certificate to this effect from the British Recruiting Office.

In his letter Laski went on to say that he had repeatedly acquainted Wing Commander James with the position but he had not received any replies to his letters.

In the House of Commons on 14 December 1943 Wing Commander James said:

May I make a purely personal apology and put on record in Hansard correction of a very unfortunate thing I said in this House a few months ago? Speaking of the personnel employed by the BBC I said that Professor Laski was an unfit person to employ because in the last war he left the country to avoid fighting. I deeply regret having made a most mischievous, misleading and wholly untrue statement. I was misinformed as Laski only left the country on the advice of his tutor at Oxford—the brother of an old friend of mine—after he had been rejected for military service. He made repeated subsequent efforts to join the Services here and abroad and was rejected. I very much regret that I should have caused him pain as I must have done. I wish to withdraw anything I said, especially because, disliking his political outlook intensely and in every respect, I am the more reluctant that he might think I made this attack because of his political views. I would like to put on record my abject apology to this House, which I misled, and to Professor Laski whom I wronged.

Readily supported by his wife, Laski was ever willing to champion the cause of birth control and he told Holmes of an incident in this connection which amused him. He said:

I went to Lincoln to speak on education and the Dean of Lincoln (Thomas Charles Fry) took the chair. During question time a man asked me how I could expect a workman to be interested in education when his first interest was to get them (his children) earning so as to keep body and soul together in the home. I said that I agreed and that there was no hope for the working class until the devastating torrent of children was somewhere and somehow stemmed. Up, stentorian-like jumped the Dean. He begged most emphatically to dissent from this pestilential doctrine. He knew many working class families which had brought up six children in decency and comfort on thirty shillings a week. It was our duty to follow the scriptural injunction and multiply as the sand upon the seashore. Voice then floats from the audience: 'Don't you fret, Mr Laski, the Dean has only two children himself.' The Dean left hurriedly amid roars of laughter.

Throughout the war Laski never lost an opportunity to urge that Labour Ministers in the Coalition Government should make the passing of socialist measures by Parliament a condition of their continued co-operation in the war effort. He used all his influence, too, to try to ensure that the Party, even during the darkest days of the war, was planning for the situation which he believed would have to be faced at the end of hostilities. Indeed, as early as May 1940, at the time of the collapse of France, he was presenting a report to the Party's annual conference expressing the view that only ownership 'by our society of the essential means of production will enable us, after the war, to move from the economics of scarcity to the economics of abundance'. And during the months which followed Laski wrote several articles for the *New Statesman* urging that the Government which the Labour leaders were supporting should introduce such socialism as was possible during the war years.

In 1941, when Herbert Morrison persuaded the Party's national executive committee to set up a new Central Committee on Reconstruction Problems, Laski readily took on the job of secretary. Other committees were formed to deal with particular aspects of post-war planning and Laski co-operated with Arthur Greenwood in the preparation of a number of important policy papers that paved the way for the document which ultimately formed the basis of the Party's programme for the 1945 General Election.

At the 1942 annual conference of the Party Laski was on his feet moving a national executive resolution affirming that there must be no return to 'an unplanned competitive society'. He told the delegates he was fully conscious of the immense services that Churchill had rendered to the nation, and through it, the world. He said he recognised and gladly acknowledged the greatness of Churchill's leadership but because he had given so much they asked him to give more. This, Laski declared, was a people's war and they wanted a pledge that he would help in a people's peace. So far, he said, Churchill had evaded the assurance; he must stand by the people of Britain not only in their war against the vested interests abroad but also in their war against vested interests at home.

But, whilst Laski was never tired of stressing that the war offered a wonderful opportunity for the bringing about of a social revolution by consent, the Labour members of the Cabinet had other priorities. They were no less anxious than Laski that there should be no return to the conditions of the 1930s but considered that the first objective was to win the war. The over-riding priority was to defeat Hitler. Ernest Bevin was a firm supporter of Attlee in this field, feeling that, simply on practical grounds, major changes could not be enacted in the middle of war and that all that could emerge would be high-sounding declarations and general promises. But to Laski the idea that victory must mean, as well as peace abroad, social justice at home, dominated much of his thinking. He addressed large and small meetings all over the country, including groups of members of the armed forces, and of the Labour members of the Government he was sometimes bitterly critical. Writing at that time to his friend Felix Frankfurter in the United States he said of proposals for reconstruction 'the critical stage will not come until the Labour ministers try to water it down so as to maintain their happy subordination to Winston'.

And when Laski decided to write direct to the Prime Minister on the subject Churchill replied: 'My dear Laski: It is entirely beyond my share of life and strength to deal with all the issues which your letter raises. In my view we ought to win the war first and then, in a free country, the issues of socialism and free enterprise can be fought out in a constitutional manner. I certainly should think it very undemocratic if anyone were to try to carry socialism during a party truce without a Parliamentary majority. I have always accounted you a friend rather than a follower. I think it will be a pity to break up the national unity in the war and that, I believe, is the opinion of the mass of the people.'

From time to time during the war Attlee answered Laski back but he persisted in his line and, in May 1944, just a month before D-day and during one of the most anxious periods of the war Attlee sat down at his typewriter and tapped out (I have seen much of what he produced in this way) a 1,300-word letter which was the measure of his desire and indeed determination, once and for all to put the position to Laski as seen by the Labour Party leaders in the Coalition Government. Here are just a couple of paragraphs:

... As I see it, your argument amounted to this, that unless our socialist principles had been by the end of the war put into force, there would be a repetition of the disaster of 1919. If this is so then obviously all of us in the party who support the maintenance of this government in power in order to win the war are making ourselves responsible with our eyes open to bringing the world to disaster. The logic of that position would be that we should at once break the coalition and seek for a general election now in the hope of getting a Socialist majority. Hence my comment, So what? But the Executive only a short time ago voted strongly for continuing the present government in power. The party is strongly and rightly insistent that the government should make provision now for the interim period. But it is obvious that given these two things that preparation cannot be based entirely on socialist principles or entirely on capitalist principles. There is inevitably a compromise.

... At the present time I am engaged for a good many hours a day on postwar problems which cover a very wide range from detailed matters of our internal economy to the widest matters of international political and economic import. I discuss these with my colleagues and endeavour naturally to get as much of our policy accepted, and I find on many matters more agreement than you would perhaps expect, but on other matters I may have to accept a compromise. Why? Because for better or worse this country has got to play a big part in shaping the postwar settlement, and geographically and also ideologically we are situated between the USSR and the USA. I believe that it is of primary importance for the peace of the world that these three great powers should work in harmony. It is, therefore, necessary that we should discuss with them both the immediate and the longer-distance problems of the peace, and we cannot do that if we cannot come to some understanding among ourselves.

During the whole of his political life Laski was conscious of the distrust of 'intellectuals' felt, and indeed expressed, by some trade union and Labour Party leaders. He had plenty of evidence over the years of the real affection that the rank and file of the movement had for him but he worried sometimes about the uncertainty that was occasionally openly expressed as to his motives and understanding of problems. Owing to the illness of Ellen Wilkinson,

Laski was chairman of the 1944 annual conference of the Labour Party and in the course of his presidential address he said:

Your chairman today is an example of that dangerous species who, so far as my knowledge goes, is in our movement rarely trusted and never praised, the species whose professional work is criticism and thought... I represent something a little different from the past, British by birth, middle class by origin, Jewish by inheritance,— symbolic of the vital fact that the Labour Party knows no boundaries save those which are defined by faith in its principles and policies.

CHAPTER FOUR

AMERICA — INDIA — ISRAEL

I recall that when Laski, on visiting Ruskin College, Oxford, to speak to a group of young trade unionists, said he had chosen to talk about America, many of his audience were momentarily disappointed. He was at the height of his career as a political scientist and very active in the Labour Party and we had hoped that he would be dealing with current issues in our own country. However, he had not been speaking for more than a few minutes before we realised we were in for a treat. For nearly three-quarters of an hour he held us almost spellbound with a review of some of the aspects of United States' life, of his own experiences in that country, and his assessment of what was likely to happen. And when he had finished we were bursting to ask questions. He had really made his subject live and as he talked he had shown us that there was a relevance between what was happening across the Atlantic and events here at home that we had never even thought of.

Although, as we have seen, Laski left the United States in 1920 in discouraging circumstances it is obvious that those four years at Harvard laid the foundations of a fascination for the country which drew him back year after year. Indeed a substantial part of his life was spent in America where he became a familiar figure at very many universities and colleges. To list them would read almost like a catalogue of the country's leading teaching institutions. During the 1939–45 war, when he did not make the journey across the Atlantic he very often felt frustrated. Writing to a friend over there he said: 'I miss America more than I can say. It's like having a piece of myself cut out. There are things I want to see and smell and feel there which at this distance seem like shadows dancing madly on a wall.'

Laski was on personal terms with distinguished American political figures as well as with men and women in the academic world and they looked forward to meeting him on his visits to their country. I have seen a note from President Franklin Roosevelt to his appointments secretary: 'I understand Harold Laski is in town. I want to have lunch with him one day next week. Please arrange.' On Laski's death Mrs Eleanor Roosevelt, recalling those days, said that she would always remember 'with pleasure and profit' their meetings, adding that 'he was one of those people who was willing to consider what other people thought and felt, though he had real convictions and the ability to express them. He never gave one the feeling of not being willing to listen to other people's ideas'. Laski was friendly with John Winant, United States Ambassador to Britain from 1941 to 1946, and on occasions drafted speeches for him. Winant, in sending him a signed photograph, said: 'You always helped me as you have so many others and I have always welcomed your criticism and your support.' On one occasion, writing from Washington to say he was about to return to London, Winant, implying that he wished to see Laski, said: 'I would like you to set me straight.'

As he went around the United States over a period covering twenty years giving lectures in public halls and speaking at universities and colleges, Laski invariably attracted large audiences not only because of what he had to say but because he was a nationally-known controversial figure, ever ready to develop the thinking behind his strongly-held socialist principles. Katherine Keene was a student at the University of Washington in 1939 and she has told me of the controversy when Laski was engaged as a visiting professor there. She said:

> There was considerable excitement before he came. The money had been put up for a series of lectures—on 'Problems of Modern Government' from a fund left by a man who made a fortune in the lumbering industry and was a director of several banks, and the notion that the socialist Laski would be financed from capitalist funds was too much for some people. Efforts were made to have his appointment rescinded but the University President stood by his Political Science Department, and Laski came, the University newspaper having as its headline 'At Long Laski!'

Amongst observations (as reported in the Press) by opponents of the Laski lectures were: 'We have enough trouble at the

University without importing Mr Laski from England to stir up some more. . . . Laski comes over here with his panacea for solving our troubles while at the same time our country is feeding his. . . . The University campus should not be a springboard for any subversive doctrines.' When the first lecture took place there was a crowd estimated at over three thousand, and the morning after one Washington paper reported 'scores of people were turned away when the auditorium was filled. Some took seats in the gallery of the building which has been condemned as unsafe and refused to leave when requested by a campus marshall'.

Whilst the American press generally never lost an opportunity to remind readers that Laski was a socialist—with all that that meant—there were those in the United States who especially welcomed him because of his political convictions and sought his services as a speaker. And not all his advocacy of socialism and criticism of aspects of capitalism was done in open public meetings. He went considerably out of his way to meet men and women with 'left' views on both informal social occasions and at private meetings and seminars. Herbert Aptheker, now Director of the American Institute for Marxist Studies, recounted to me something of the atmosphere of those days and of the lively arguments that used to take place. 'And remember', he told me, 'that whilst the majority of Americans thought of Harold Laski as very "left" politically there were others, I was one of them, who thought he wasn't left enough in his views.'

I talked with a man in the reference department of the New York Library who recalled going to one of Laski's political meetings and of asking a question at the conclusion of his speech. He told me that when the meeting was formally concluded Laski stepped down from the platform to inquire if the questioner was satisfied with the answer he had been given. 'For about a quarter of an hour', I was told, 'Laski earnestly developed the points he had made from the platform in answer to my question. He was so anxious to help me and that I should understand his thinking that he asked for my name and address. A few weeks later I had a letter from him which he had written on his return to England with which he enclosed a number of pamphlets which he felt might interest me. That was nearly thirty years ago but I have never forgotten his kindness.'

Shortly after the initial lecture of his 1939 American tour Laski developed a throat infection and, whilst he spent a few days in bed, Mrs Laski gave an interview to the newspapers. Asked what she thought of the controversy which had developed, she said: 'My husband is a serious man. He thinks the world is in chaos and he wants to put it right. Some people hear the word 'Marxist' and they think it is Communism. My husband is only trying to make people think even if they do disagree.' It was reported that for the occasion of the interview Mrs Laski: 'Had on a bright green wool dress, loose English cut, that brought out the red cast in her hair. The colour of her hair had no political portent, she said, adding that her husband's beard would also be red if he had to stay in bed much longer without shaving.' When questioned about the fee her husband was getting for the lecture tour, Mrs Laski was reported as saying: 'We don't eat the money. With what my husband has earned in this country he's been able to send eleven thousand dollars for refugees in Spain and he's been able to get out of Germany I don't know how many refugees. My husband and I are not socialists on the platform and capitalists at home.' Whilst giving a lecture later in the tour Laski referred to his having developed a sore throat which he described as 'quincy'. Never at a loss to associate himself with distinguished people he reminded his audience that 'George Washington had died of quincy'.

It has often been commented that Laski could speak for a considerable period without notes and never hesitate for a word or a phrase, but this did not mean that he had always spent time thinking about what he was going to say and preparing himself for the occasion. His American friend Felix Frankfurter has given a typical example of the way in which Laski could speak 'off the cuff', as the saying is.

The occasion was a lecture at the Ford Hall in Boston and on the way by taxi from Frankfurter's home to the meeting-place he asked Laski: 'Harold, what are you going to talk about?' 'Oh', came the reply, 'a critique of our economic system.' When Frankfurter expressed some uncertainty about the suitability of the subject for the occasion Laski asked: 'Well, what should I talk about?' and his host reminded him that he had recently been associated with the round-table conference on Indian affairs (attended by Gandhi and Nehru) as assistant to Lord Chancellor Sankey who had presided. 'Why not tell them about the complexities of the problems associated with the India question?' Frankfurter suggested and Laski answered: 'All right'.

'By that time', Frankfurter has left it on record, 'we had arrived at Ashburton Place where Ford Hall was. I was to be chairman that night. That's all the preliminary talk there was to that extraordinary performance of his. I don't know who else could have achieved it on either side of the Atlantic. It was then nearly eight o'clock, and in no time I had to be on my feet and introduce Professor Laski. There he stood, each hand on the lapel of his coat—no gesture—and for one hour he delivered an address on India which could have been taken down and published in book form without correcting anything—all these long sentences and all these qualifying phrases in apple-pie order. To be sure he was loaded. He had lived with this subject for several months or years, if you will, but that kind of quick mobilisation of your knowledge and the capacity to put it out with such architectural completeness and finished beauty of speech was a feat of the highest order.'

I have been given many examples, too, of Laski's remembering everything he had written after preparing an address. There was the occasion when, invited to give his lecture, he handed his manuscript to the chairman of the meeting as he got up to speak and then delivered the whole lecture word perfect just as he had previously written it down.

One of the characteristics that endeared Laski to his American audiences was the frank way he dealt with questions. Charles Odell, of the Pennsylvania Bureau of Employment Security, has recalled for me an example of this that occurred when Laski was guest lecturer at a management seminar associated with the National Institute of Public Affairs in Washington, DC. He said:

When Professor Laski had finished a very erudite analysis of the New Deal and its parallels to earlier social reforms in England, our moderator, a retired Republican Congressman named Fred Davenport, asked a loaded question: 'How does it happen, Professor Laski, that all these well-intended social reforms, like Social Security and National Health Insurance, just don't seem to accomplish in practice what was intended for them by the Congress?' Laski, without batting an eyelash, turned to Davenport and said: 'Precisely because of people like you.' Davenport was shocked and his face turned reddish purple. 'What on earth do you mean by that?' he gasped. 'Well', retorted Laski, 'first, you Republican-Conservatives try in every way to kill a good social reform by massive propaganda against it. Then you kill it with kindness when its passage is inevitable by loading it up with so many devices to protect the private interests you represent that it becomes an operational nightmare.' I have often thought since of the wisdom and insight of Professor Laski as I witnessed what has happened to such Great Society programs as Medicare, the Civil Rights Act of 1964, the Economic Opportunity Act, and many others.

An American who was a student of Laski's at the London School of Economics has recalled his visit to an obscure American college founded to secure educational opportunities irrespective of colour and political creed for all attending it. Laski could have lectured for five times the fee at any one of a dozen well-known universities but he preferred to devote his few weeks of leisure to help a struggling institution to find its feet. His reward was a gratitude on the part of the students expressed in terms not far short of adoration.

It was not unusual for Laski before returning home to England after a period as a guest lecturer to send a 'farewell message' to his hosts, and after lecturing at the University of Washington at Seattle he told them something of what he had gained from his stay with them. He said:

No teacher who has had even a tithe of the kindness that I have experienced, alike from colleagues and students in the University of Washington, can avoid a sense of humility before the obligation it creates. Seattle has given me a wealth of new experience; the sense of a new world of whose existence I had before no more than that dim awareness one gains from books. I leave it realising how incomplete my vision of America would have been had I not seen this endless empire of the Pacific North-West, with its immense resources, its still living spirit of the pioneers, its hunger to understand the complicated world in whose intricacies it is so inescapably involved. May it have the wisdom in the coming years to face its problems with insight and with courage.

Naturally enough, my main preoccupation in Seattle has been with the University and its problems. What an immense opportunity. There is nowhere, as far as I know, in the United States a student-body more eager for knowledge or more ready to respond to the best that University life can offer. The central issue the University confronts is how adequately to offer its students the chance they deserve. It will not be easy. It means more freedom for teacher and student alike. It means more leisure for thought, more opportunity for research. It means the recognition on the part of the community that, as Edmund Burke once said, the temple of truth should be erected upon an eminence. If the citizens of Washington want their students to get from the University all that is in it to give, they must be prepared to recognise that the road to intellectual achievement lies through the highroad to freedom. They must be ready for experiment in ideas. They must recognise that a new world is being created before our eyes, and that we cannot map its frontiers without the risks of a voyage of exploration. They must be willing for the economist and the political scientist to do in the realm of ideas what Lewis and Clark did in the realm of physical discovery. And the way to make the citizens realise the urgency of this attitude is for the teacher and student alike to stand four-square against those who would make the University accept the truths of the past rather than investigate the potentialities of the future. A new idea has the same right to its welcome as a new machine. But the new idea will only come as the scholar is assured of the unfettered right freely to promulgate its substance.

Freedom for teacher and student; that is the primary necessity. And next to freedom is the realisation that true teaching is not in lectures but in the friendship of teachers and taught. The danger that confronts an institution so vast as Washington is the loss of this individual relationship through size. I would myself cheerfully sacrifice the building programme of the next decade for such a reorganisation of methods of instruction as would emphasise the principle that a university consists not of buildings but of men. The more fully that is understood the more profoundly will the scholar's spirit permeate those who pass through these academic halls. I know how difficult it is for the outsider to academic life to realise the truth. Let him remember that Paris and Oxford, Bologna and Cambridge had no board of trustees, no catalogue, no athletics, few outside activities, beyond the constant communion between their scholars and their students, in medieval time. Yet men journeyed all over Western Europe for the chance to work there with a great scholar. So it could be too in Washington; if its masters are imaginative enough to be willing to pay the price.

Granted that willingness, I think the University here has the chance of a great future. The North-West can be a pivotal area in the coming history of America; it has the resources and it has the men. It needs only the wisdom to use them to the full advantage. There is a city of letters, not 'built of hands, the path from which leads to the stars'. If that city be built in the State of Washington, if its spirit preside over the University which might be its central fortress, the years to come may well be the seed-time of a great age of creativeness. Certainly no one will watch its development with more eagerness or hope than one who has been so generously welcomed as I into what is best in this fellowship.

During his many journeys across the Atlantic, Laski generally managed to get on good terms with at least a few of his fellow-passengers, and Stuart Whibley, now eighty-six and living in Bridgnorth, has told me that during the 1930s, on his way to the United States, he found himself, quite by accident, seated with Laski at a table for two on the outward-bound Cunard liner. He said:

After our first meal together Laski asked if I had anything to read and took me to his cabin where he showed me an imposing row of at least twenty new books. He explained that they were a gift from his publishers who had learned of his trip. Our political outlooks were utterly opposed but as a travelling companion Laski was unrivalled. He knew everyone and everything and one forgave his obvious conceit in his own brilliance because of the delight and interest in his anecdotes and conversation, however one-sided. Although going to America mainly on a lecture-tour he said that, on leaving the ship, he was going to Washington 'to stay with Franklin and Eleanor' as he put it, as the President and his wife were old friends. As we approached New York Laski said he feared the press would come out by launch before we docked to interview him. To avoid this he asked me to head them off with excuses while he hid in a lavatory.

By good fortune for me, Laski and I returned to England on the same ship and again we shared a table. When we came down to breakfast on 1 May we found the steward had decorated the white table-cloth by spreading around a number of small hammer and sickle emblems cut out of red paper. I asked Laski why the steward made such a fuss of him. He said he had a cousin who was a director of Marks & Spencers. It appeared that when Cunard stewards were nearing the end of their sea-going employment they got in touch with Laski who sent their names to his cousin who gave them employment. I remember two other happenings on that crossing. Laski knew another passenger, Jan Hamburg, the violinist and brother of the pianist Mark Hamburg. On several evenings Jan would invite us to his cabin and play to us. Laski and I were travelling 'tourist' but after dinner one night he said he was going to the 'first class' to see some friends. When he returned he flourished a cheque for £5,000 given to him by a lady for Jewish charities in which he was interested.

One of the American links which Laski maintained and treasured over the years was with the Kennedy family. John Kennedy, who became President of the United States, was a student of his at the London School of Economics in 1935–36, and his elder brother Joseph (killed in World War II) was there two years earlier. Many people were surprised that their father, a wealthy man and a strong supporter of the capitalist system (he was US Ambassador to Britain from 1938 to 1941) should send his sons to the School and particularly to study under Laski. It was Joseph junior, who—as I have said—came to London first, and his mother, Mrs Rose Fitzgerald Kennedy, has set out the reason in her memoirs, published under the title *Times to Remember*. She said:

> I must say I was rather taken aback by his choice. I asked Joe why he chose the London School of Economics in favour of sending Joe Junior to Oxford or Cambridge to study under renowned professors at those two great and famous places? After all, Joe was by that time—1933—quite a well-known capitalist. His answers, which puzzled me then, make perfect sense now. The United States and most of the Western world were in the grip of the Depression, and there were many revolutionary currents and ideas—Marxist and semi-Marxist—in the political atmosphere. Roosevelt had taken office and the New Deal had barely begun. It was still unformulated, and no one could be sure whether the new Administration would succeed in restoring stability and a sense of confidence in the free-enterprise system. Therefore, he wanted our son to understand the challenges he might be facing as put forth by a brilliant challenger, Professor Laski. He already had the same plan in mind for Jack. For after all, he said 'These boys are going to have a little money when they get older, and they should know what the "have nots" are thinking and planning'. As he said later in an interview, speaking of Professor Laski: 'I disagreed with everything he wrote ... but I never taught the boys to disapprove of someone just because I didn't accept his ideas. They heard enough from me, and I decided they should be exposed to someone of intelligence and vitality on the other side.'

When, after the war, John Kennedy was writing a book about his late brother—he called it *As We Remember Joe*—he asked Laski to comment on his brother as he knew him at the School. Laski wrote:

> A large part of every teacher's life is in the students for whom he feels a special affection; and when they die, something in him, I

think, dies too. Joe came to work with me at the London School of Economics and Political Science in 1933–34, for the year before he entered Harvard. He was adorably young and still more adorably unsophisticated. He went to some seven or eight lectures a week and did a weekly essay for me; and he accompanied my wife and me when I went to lecture at the University of Moscow in the summer of 1934.

Three things, above all, stand out in my recollection of young Joe in that year. Above all his astonishing vitality. He was interested in everything and only disturbed by the limitations of twenty-four hours which nature has put on the day. And second, there was his astonishing capacity for enthusiasm. What he liked, he liked with all his heart. He had nothing of the cynic's pose which sometimes affects the undergraduate. He gave all of himself to what he did with immense energy and eagerness. The third thing was his profound interest in politics. He had set his heart on a political career; he had often sat in my study and submitted with that smile that was pure magic to relentless teasing about his determination to be nothing less than President of the United States.

At the stage when Joe worked with me, of course, his mind was only just beginning to discover the enchantment of thought. But his essays were written with great care, and he took criticism with a disarming friendliness. He never stopped asking questions. I had him join a seminar of mine which was intended for third-year students; and I can see now the quick shift of his attention as the argument moved from one undergraduate to another.... He was very popular with the other students. He was so simple and so frank and so forthright. They loved to tease him about his American ways, and I think he enjoyed being teased if only because the process enabled him to affirm, with that special kind of laughter that has intense conviction behind, his love for America.... He never posed. He was always anxious to know. He repaid one's efforts with a fidelity of heart that was deeply moving. I am glad I knew Joe....

Although Laski remained on good terms with the Kennedy family after the boys had returned to the United States he refused in 1939 to write an introduction to the first book written by John Kennedy, then a twenty-three-year-old Harvard graduate. The book, *Why England Slept*, which became a best-seller, was written as a thesis and dealt with this country's lack of military preparation on the eve of World War II. It was John Kennedy's father—by that time US Ambassador at the Court of St James—who had asked Laski to write the introduction but he refused because he said it was the product of 'an immature mind'. He added that 'if it hadn't been written by the son of a very rich man he wouldn't have found a publisher'. In the event, the introduction was written by Henry Luce, the magazine publisher, who said that if John Kennedy was characteristic of the younger generation 'many of us would be happy to have the destinies of this republic handed over to this generation at once'. The year after the war ended, when John Kennedy was on a visit to this country, he told Laski: 'You were quite right about the book.'

At the height of the war, in mid-1942, Laski had an invitation from Mrs Roosevelt to speak at an International Students Service Assembly in Washington, the purpose of which, she said, was to bring together young people from various countries. He was invited to stay with the President and his wife at the White House and, as may be imagined, Laski was eager to accept. However, some time before he had said he would not go to the United States during hostilities unless it was to perform some sort of war work and, although he had no need to (he could easily have got a priority passage on the strength of Mrs Roosevelt's invitation), he asked for Churchill's approval. All this happened at a time when Laski was publicly criticising the Prime Minister's 'out-dated outlook' and his prejudice against socialism. Not surprisingly, Churchill, who did not want to give Laski the chance to develop his criticism across the Atlantic, withheld his approval. This was a blow to Laski who was anxious, apart from the prime reason for the visit, to meet old friends again.

Laski continued to correspond with President Roosevelt throughout the war, congratulating him on his re-election and, looking forward to the end of the war, said it would be 'unbearable if after all these years of pain and suffering and death, you did not insist that the immense power of the United States be used to lay the foundations of peace and civilised living. But I know you want to fight for this end not less than I. . . . We who care deeply for you want to see this term a memorable epoch in the history of mankind. May you have the strength and friends to end as greatly as those first magic days when you entered the White House'. In reply Roosevelt said ' . . . I feel confident that this time we shall be able to make a definite start in eliminating the constant threat of aggression and war and in bringing about international co-operation and security. . .'. When, in April 1945, just before victory in Europe, Roosevelt died Laski wrote to his friend Felix Frankfurter: 'This is a blow almost beyond words. If you knew how much I had counted on him for the first years of peace. It is hardly a fortnight since I had a grand and cheerful letter from him. I can hardly bear to think that I shall never see him again.'

Laski took an especial interest in the Roosevelt College in Chicago, founded by friends and admirers of the late US President. Established to provide university education on a strictly non-discriminating basis, Laski endeavoured to give a course of lectures there on each of his visits and he also did what he could to interest friends in the project.

Some idea of Laski's standing in the United States may be judged from the fact that, when in the spring of 1947, it was planned to establish a Jewish-sponsored co-educational university, Laski was invited to become its first president.

The offer was made in a letter from Albert Einstein, the physicist. Otto Nathan, an economist of New York, a close friend of Einstein, executor of Einstein's will and one of the two trustees of his literary estate, has recounted the circumstances to me. Einstein wrote to Laski telling him that it was hoped the new university would make it easier for young men and women of Jewish faith and of other minorities to obtain a first-class education. Similarly, it was hoped that the project would help scientists and scholars who, under conditions prevailing at that time, suffered from grave discrimination in finding a place where they could teach and work. Moreover, the new university would not discriminate against anyone on account of sex, colour, creed, national origin or political opinion.

Einstein told Laski that whoever would be appointed first president of the university would have the challenging task of helping in the basic foundation of the institution and of selecting the initial faculty on which so much depended. Laski was told that the view was commonly held that he was the man who, accepting the great challenge, was most likely to succeed. Not only was he familiar with the United States and her academic institutions, but he was an outstanding scholar with a world-wide reputation. To make it easier for Laski to accept the invitation it was suggested that he might become president for, say, the first two or three all-important years.

Dr Nathan told me that Laski pointed out in his reply it was important for political reasons that he remain in England. The new university was opened in 1948 at Waltham, Massachusetts, and was named Brandeis University after Louis Brandeis, the first Jew in history to be appointed a Justice of the United States Supreme Court in 1916.

It was in 1949 that Laski went to the United States for the last time. He travelled under the auspices of the Sidney Hillman Foundation, a fund established to honour the much-revered leader of the Amalgamated Clothing Workers' Union. In this way he was able to give a number of lectures which were later collected and published under the title *Trade Unions in the New Society*. Laski welcomed the invitation not only because it gave him yet another opportunity to visit the country but because it enabled him to pay tribute to a man who was an established trade union leader when Laski was a young instructor at Harvard. He said: 'I learned much from him during the next thirty years' and he dedicated the collected lectures to a man who, as a national trade union leader, 'made one of the vital if inadequately recognised contributions to the great effort which, after Pearl Harbour, made America that arsenal of democracy without which, as Marshall Stalin himself admitted, the united nations would have lost the Second World War'.

Unfortunately Laski's last visit to the United States coincided with a bitter dispute in academic circles arising from the dismissal of some Washington University professors after an inquiry into their allegedly left-wing convictions. Laski said the sackings had taken place 'in circumstances of indefensible insult' and whilst he was most cordially welcomed at some colleges, the tour was marred by outbursts of intolerance and opposition and reactionary groups forced the abandonment of lectures at California and Washington. However, the wheel of Fate had turned full circle since the events of 1920, and Harvard came to the rescue and cordially invited Laski to give the banned lectures at Cambridge.

These prejudices gave Laski very considerable concern. He referred to four university professors who considered themselves obliged to refrain from publishing a history of industrial relations in their State being concerned that, in the prevailing climate, it might put their very continued employment at risk. He commented that the situation was such that it was 'unwise for Americans to write books or articles on issues about which there are deep divisions of opinion unless the writer refuses to take sides or accepts the orthodox view'. He said that American opinion was putting in jeopardy the right to speak openly, commenting that 'nothing is more dangerous in academic life than a situation where teachers, whose function is the discovery of new knowledge and the communication of insight they have wrested, stand uncertain whether to speak at all'. In a sentence, he felt that academic freedom was 'closely linked with the teacher's right to leave his ivory tower and relate his specialism with life'. Not long before Laski died his opinion was sought by an ex-student as to whether a permanent teaching post in the United States should be accepted. Sadly, he said: 'Do you know, I could not bear to teach at an American college today if I did not know that there was always a ship at New York on which I could come home.' I recall an American student telling me that, at the end of his term at the London School of Economics and before returning home, Laski gave him a letter of commendation which he greatly appreciated. 'I was, however', he told me, 'afraid to use it when seeking employment because school boards might know Laski as "a socialist type".'

It was in the course of his lectures given under the auspices of the Hillman Foundation that Laski stressed to American audiences the impossibility of separating the political from the economic significance of trade union action. He argued that they should be linked in order to be really effective and gave a number of examples to make his point. Part of these lectures were concerned with the problems thrown up by the relations of organised labour with the State (both in America and Britain) and the attitude of Governments to it. Incidentally, particularly in view of current thinking in some sections of the British trade union movement on the subject of 'industrial democracy' (and the call for worker participation by having seats on supervisory boards) it is interesting to find Laski saying it is 'obviously unsatisfactory to select trade union leaders for important executive posts in management when the ownership of an industry becomes public instead of private. Even more it is unsatisfactory to accept men chosen by and responsible to the trade unions upon the committees of management; they then would be in a position where conflicting loyalties would gravely impair the clarity of the decisions they would have to take'.

Of the score of books Laski wrote, only two were specially devoted to American themes. There was *The American Presidency* which appeared in 1940, and a 760-page volume, *The American Democracy* published eight years later. His book on the Presidency was dedicated 'with deep affection and respect' to President Roosevelt and was welcomed as a 'lively contribution to a highly significant topic, presenting a clear study of that strange amalgam of monarchy and parliamentarism, the Presidency of the United States'.

American Democracy, a commentary on, and an interpretation of, United States economics, political, social and cultural institutions, was well received although some uncertainty was expressed as to the up-to-dateness of some parts. I have seen it referred to as 'one of the greatest books ever written on America' and ranking 'in many scholarly American minds as one of the three greatest studies of American democracy by foreigners—or by Americans for that matter—the other two being de Tocqueville's *Democracy in America* and Lord Bryce's *The American Commonwealth*'. Commentators agreed that the volume 'repaid study' and gave as much insight into the mind of the observer as the minds of those observed.

Of the Church in the United States, Laski was critical, not surprisingly, of course, in view of his attitude to religion generally. He said: 'Indeed the more they emphasise their view that only eternal values are really important, the more, however unconsciously, they are really preaching submission to the powers that be.' He said: 'The American churches produce religiosity and not religion' and 'so far from the churches permeating America with the religious spirit, America has permeated the churches with the spirit of the successful man.

Looking at life generally, Laski said in his book that Americans are 'so hostile to tradition in all superficial matters and so deeply conservative in all fundamental notions', and, developing the point he said:

> They are at once a practical and experimental people in the things of everyday life and enjoy innovation in that realm, while they are a curiously conservative people in the realm of fundamental ideas. They accept a revolution like the coming of the motor car or the

aeroplane without any difficulty as a natural change. To require, on the other hand, that they adapt themselves to a new assumption about the Constitution, or the character of slavery as a Southern institution, or the pathetic fallacy of Liberal Christianity, is an extraordinarily difficult matter.

On the political parties of the United States, as they functioned in his day, he said:

The political party in America does not think; it has no vital philosophic doctrine. It buys the doctrine from one group or another on the gamble that the sum of the doctrines it buys will add up to enough votes to keep it in power, nationally or locally. That is why it never proceeds directly to a defined goal but is always weighing pressures against one another in the effort to see where and how it can make the best bargain.

But his fundamental admiration and indeed affection for the country keeps breaking through. He wrote:

I love America.... A large part of the disasters of Europe has been the outcome of the simple fact that men have preferred power to justice. You are a people who still have what is in large part denied to ourselves. You are a people who still can fulfil the dream with which you started. You are an experimental civilisation. Your resources are still magnificent and unexhausted. You shatter those grim traditions that make the relationship of classes as static and as stereotyped as they are with ourselves ... with you there is a certain spaciousness and a certain exhilaration.

It was appreciated that Laski had 'tried to see and depict this complex democracy as a whole, without over-simplifying, without evading. He has not forced facts into the pattern required by some theory or some doctrine. And if the result is not some nice, neat "interpretation" of it all so much the better'. As Laski himself said 'there is so much more in America than any one man can know. There is so much in it, both of beauty and ugliness, of good and evil, that he cannot put it into words'.

Although Laski, towards the end, might have been increasingly critical of some United States institutions and attitudes of those in authority he never lost his deep love of the country. When he returned home for the last time, in the spring of 1949, he used the phrase 'enchanted days' to describe how he felt about his visit. He used to like in his correspondence and talks with friends, to refer to the academic institutions he had visited (there were few of which he did not have particular memories) and to think that they, too, in turn, remembered him. He was anxious that his American friends should know how much they meant to him and how very little differences about politics and social philosophy really mattered.

And Laski continued to reach across the Atlantic by his frequent contributions to a series of journals which included *The Nation*, the *Atlantic Monthly*, *Harper's Magazine* and the *New Republic*. He never forgot how American journals had given him a platform in the days when, at Harvard, he was struggling for recognition. His articles, too, were syndicated in American newspapers and it is not surprising that he was known right across the vast country and that they brought him letters which he was always at pains to answer. To one American correspondent who said he hoped that Laski would not mind being reminded of when and where they had met, he replied: 'I don't often quote Shakespeare but I can honestly say that:

> I count myself in nothing else so happy
> As in a soul remembering my good friends.

Krishna Menon, who was appointed Indian High Commissioner in London when his country gained independence in 1947, was ever ready to acknowledge his indebtedness to Laski. A political science student at the London School of Economics, he obtained his BSc degree with first-class honours in 1927 at the age of thirty-one, went on to study law, and was called to the bar at the Middle Temple.

The son of a wealthy lawyer, Menon was born in Calicut, in Southern India, in 1896 and came to London (after some time as a social worker in Madras) intending to qualify as a teacher. He was, however, deeply concerned with the plight of the people of India and felt there was misunderstanding in Britain about the aspirations of his country for self-government. He soon became closely involved in the work of the India League which was actively campaigning for dominion status, and leaving a teaching post in Hertfordshire, he began his studies at the London School of Economics. He thus came under the influence of Laski who shaped his thinking and approach to the issues on which he felt so deeply. Menon found, to his delight, that Laski not only shared his belief in the justice of India's claims but was prepared to be outspoken in his views. He therefore lost no time in using the professor's standing to give prestige and authority to the cause he had at heart.

As time went on Menon gave more and more attention to his political work. His scholarships ran out, he became estranged from his family, cut himself off from their affluence, and for the next twenty years he lived the life of an exile in London, concentrating on the cause that dominated his whole life. Menon's academic qualifications would have ensured him a successful career in Britain or in India, too, where he summarily turned down a chance to become lecturer in political science at Lucknow University. With a lack of financial resources Menon became under-nourished, indeed, ill. He spent almost all his waking hours in the office of the India League, lived on cups of tea and buns, often slept only two or three hours a night, and all he could afford in the way of accommodation was a garret in the St Pancras district of London.

Obsessed to the exclusion of everything else with India's cause it is not surprising that Menon's long hours at his desk, living conditions and lack of proper food led to a complete breakdown. Laski's widow, Frida, has vividly recalled to me how, in 1938, she and her husband discovered where Menon was living, made their way to his attic room and found him bedridden and in what she described as 'a really dreadful state'. Mrs Laski told me how they talked Menon out of his almost suicidal mood and gradually got him back on his feet again. His health, however, was permanently affected.

The outbreak of war in 1939 meant no relaxation of effort on the part of Menon. Although active in the field of civil defence, he became, if it were possible, even more withdrawn and—to put it mildly—more undiplomatic in his dealings with those around him, a trait that characterised Menon's relations with people throughout his life. Laski, however, he continued to hold in a special corner of his heart and he persuaded him to be the principal speaker at a mass meeting in St Pancras Town Hall towards the end of 1945 when Menon felt that the recently-elected Labour Government was not making the progress it should towards granting independence to India. To a packed audience Laski made a speech that thrilled his one-time student and earned wild applause. Laski said: 'When are we going to realise our sense of responsibility towards the Indian people? Indian freedom is inevitable and inescapable and what we have to decide is whether that freedom shall come gracefully by British co-operation or, instead, by British hostility. We have to decide whether we are capable as a Labour Party and a Labour movement of moving forward swiftly to the proud day when we can claim that we have assisted in the emancipation of a great civilisation. We have to make up our minds. A Labour Party which is unwilling to play its full part in the emancipation of India will, sooner or later, be unwilling to play its full part in the emancipation of the British working class'.

As we all know, India gained her independence in August 1947 under the Attlee Government. Menon's dream was realised and it was a proud day for him when he was appointed Indian High Commissioner in London and became the representative of his country at the Court of St James. Later, like a fairy story come true, the man who had been living in St Pancras in extreme poverty was made a Freeman of the Borough. He was only the second to be so honoured; the first was George Bernard Shaw.

Before Menon left London in 1952 to join the Upper House of the India Parliament and enter the Cabinet, Laski was dead but Menon, who had visited him in hospital and was at Laski's bedside shortly before he died, always revered his memory. Mrs Laski told me that whenever, in later years, Menon revisited London he never failed to call on her, however pressed he was for time. The last occasion they met was only six months before Menon died, at the age of seventy-seven, in October 1974, in New Delhi.

I think it would be true to say that, next to Great Britain and the United States, nowhere is Laski's memory more revered than in India. Very many hundreds of young men and women from that country came under his influence at the London School of Economics and some of them have told me that, at the time, they really felt he took an especial interest not only in their studies but in their personal needs such as proper accommodation, financial problems, and difficulties associated with an environment far different from that in which many of them had been brought up. They have told me how patient he was when, maybe at week-ends or during vacations, they had felt the need to telephone him at his home regarding something that had suddenly arisen on which they wanted his advice.

An Indian student of Laski's has said:

> I recall how, as a new student meeting him for the first time in his room at the School he quickly put me at ease. It was my first time abroad and I was a very naïve student of economics and politics amongst the School's 'firebrands' of 1933. And yet Professor Laski gave me the feeling that my views on affairs of the day were of the utmost importance to him. His recognition of each individual student was no mere gesture or pretence at cordiality. The effort to recognise each student as a whole or complete personality was sincere. There was never a trace of condescension. Differences of opinion were respected as were differences of background, nationality, race and creed. We soon understood each other deeply and affectionately.

The seventh anniversary of the granting of self-government to India was marked in Ahmedabad, in Western India, by the founding of the Harold Laski Institute of Political Science. The inaugural address was given by G. V. Mavalankar, first Speaker of the India Parliament. His son, Purushottan Ganesh Mavalankar (who did post-graduate research work at the London School of Economics) and his wife Purnma had been prime movers in the project and they have continued to take a keen interest in its administration. Besides having reference and lending libraries and reading-rooms, regular talks and seminars are arranged. The point has been made that the Institute is in no way involved with or limited to Laski's ideas. It was, I was told, named after him 'to pay homage to an illustrious citizen of the world who was a sincere friend of India and rendered valuable assistance to us in our struggle for independence'. P. G. Mavalankar has told me that after Laski's death Mrs Laski continued to extend the hand of friendship, readily providing long-term accommodation for him and his wife at her London home.

Krishna Menon was unable to be present at the opening of the Laski Institute at Ahmedabad but he sent a message to the assembled audience which read: 'Much of what Professor Laski did to help students, and his insistence on justice and fair play will remain unknown except to the recipients. His unbounded affection and generosity of mind and heart and his sense of concern are characteristics which give him a unique place among great teachers. Professor Laski's life has been the moral foundation on which many of those who really knew him and loved him have sought to build the essential structure of their thinking and social values. His great qualities of heart, mind and personality affected them more than they knew or can assess even now.'

At the unveiling of a portrait of Laski in the Institute in 1957 Gurmukh Nihal Singh, Governor of Rajasthan, made a comment that must find an echo in many hearts in India and elsewhere. He said: 'In spite of his political and other public preoccupations and his great contribution to practical politics and to the British and international Labour movements, Professor Laski's claim to greatness and to posterity's gratitude must rest ultimately on his work as a teacher and his contribution to political thought and institutions.' After her husband's death in 1950, Mrs Laski maintained contacts with India and visited the country on two occasions, once in connection with a family planning project and once in support of the 'War on Want' campaign.

Laski's interest in India had been first awakened in 1931 when he was closely associated with the work of the unsuccessful Round Table Conference in London. Presided over by his friend the Lord Chancellor, he worked well with Lord Sankey as his assistant, and the experience had given him a deep understanding of the country's problems. Ever afterwards he had been ready to address India League meetings, and his speeches (in which he criticised the British Raj) had helped to give him the considerable standing in India which we have seen he had. It is not surprising that he was looked on by some people as one of the architects of the country's freedom and not long after India achieved independence a well-known Indian political leader declared: 'There is a vacant chair at every cabinet meeting in India. It is reserved for the ghost of Professor Harold Laski.'

That declaration was recalled for me by Norman Palmer, now Professor of Political Science at the University of Pennsylvania, who said that on frequent visits to India over the years he continued to be impressed by Laski's lasting influence. 'He had lots of disciples there,—and still has', he told me.

When the Round Table Conference on India ended, Mahatma Gandhi stayed on in London for a brief period and Leonard Woolf has told of an incident involving Laski that made a deep impression on him. Gandhi had expressed a wish to meet some Labour people and discuss with them the line of action he should take. For this purpose a Labour MP, James Horrabin, invited about a dozen well-known Labour personalities ('nearly all of us "intellectuals" not first-line politicians') and Woolf tells in his autobiography *Downhill All the Way* that

> Gandhi said that he was not going to talk much himself. He had asked us to come because he felt that the end of the Round Table Conference had left him personally in a difficult position and he was not at all clear what line he should follow when he got back to India. He wanted us each in turn to tell him how we saw the situation and what we thought his immediate course of action should be. Then one after the other round the room each said his piece. I cannot say that I found my piece very easy or illuminating. When we had all said our say there followed one of the most brilliant pyrotechnic displays which I have ever listened to. Gandhi thanked us and said that it would greatly help him if his friend Harold Laski, who was one of us, would try to sum up the various lines of judgement and advice which had emerged. Harold stood up in front of the fireplace and gave the most lucid, faultless summary of the complicated, diverse expositions of ten or fifteen people to which he had been listening in the previous hour and a half. He spoke for about twenty minutes; he gave a perfect sketch of the pattern into which the various statements and opinions logically composed themselves; he never hesitated for a word or a thought, and, as far as I could see, he never missed a point. There was a kind of beauty in his exposition, a flawless certainty and simplicity which one feels in some works of art.

Indian interest in Laski has continued and in 1970 the Harold Laski Institute at Ahmedabad asked Mr Yaakov Morris, Israeli Consul in Bombay, to talk to them about Laski and Israel. Readily accepting the invitation he said that before Israel's formal proclamation as a sovereign State on 14 May 1948 Laski was not actively involved in the Zionist movement during the critical days of struggle between it and the British Government. For many years he had kept his distance, partly due to ideological reservations and partly because of his involvement in British political life. It was only after the terrible news reached England that the Nazis had really murdered six million Jews was there a change in Laski's attitude to the movement of Jewish national liberation. Laski was a profoundly human man, highly sensitive to the sufferings of his fellow beings, and his ideological reservations about Jewish nationalism could not withstand the assault of the emotional shock waves generated by Hitler's slaughter.

Morris said that these reservations had stemmed from the very English roots of Laski's culture and consciousness. That he had been born a Jew, the son of people with a long and distinctive history, had played scarcely a role in differentiating him—in his mind and that of others—from other Englishmen. 'Jewishness' to him, as to many scientific socialists of Jewish origin was but a religious—not an ethnic—phenomenon. Laski took it for granted that he was a member of the English and not the Jewish people. His passionate love of England, its history and civilisation, all the more enrooted because of his attachment to its socialist and Labour traditions, precluded such a second involvement and loyalty. Until Hitler, therefore, Laski's Jewishness had been no problem; it had been but an accident of birth. Morris went on:

Mass murder of Jews by Hitler, therefore, came to men like Harold Laski as a double shock. Not only did it reveal the capacity of what was considered a 'civilised' nation to become a nation of acquiescent or active butchers—a nation which but yesterday had had a powerful reformist and revolutionary Labour movement; it also raised in its most stark and merciless form the special problem of the Jews. For regardless as to whether they had been religious or not, whether they had been socialists, liberals or capitalists, whether they had considered themselves ethnic Jews or assimilated Germans, all of the six million had been fed to the ovens *as Jews*. Socialists like Laski had believed that with the overthrow of capitalism the Jewish problem—which they had misread as anti-semitism and not homelessness—would be solved automatically. Hitler had demonstrated that for the Jew, as no other, dependence upon the victory of socialism might find every Jew dead before that victory was achieved. The non-Jewish worker or peasant might lose the battle for socialism temporarily and rise in revolt again; the Jew, however, whether worker or middle-class, could not be resurrected from the ashes of the crematoria.

The shock of the news from Europe, therefore, was of a two-fold nature to Harold Laski. Emotionally, it was impossible to absorb the fact of six million murders. Ideologically, to a socialist of Jewish origin who had thought of himself as nothing but an Englishman, the spectacle of a third of the Jewish people being destroyed without the ability to defend itself, or without the ability of the socialist movement to prevent its destruction, raised a most profound, and unanswered question. 'Has any socialist the right to condemn an entire people to dependence upon others, or upon the success or failure of socialism with other peoples?' Assimilation might be the solution for individual Jews, but if the Jewish masses survive as a people of Jews, is not the solution—as for other people—one of self-determination? If it is to be self-determination, however, then this series of Jewish minority pockets, scattered among the nations of the world, must surely be gathered together upon a territory of its own where—as other nations—it can be sovereign, determine its own economy and culture, defend its physical existence, and—if conquered—rise in revolt again.

Morris said he recalled how troubled Laski was by the Nazi German experience. For the first time he faced the problem of his own identity. The German socialist of Jewish origin had never questioned the fact that he was a German until Hitler singled him out, not as a socialist but as a Jew. Could this not happen in any capitalist country where a Jewish minority existed? Could the Jews not fight for socialism as a people more effectively on their own territory than as a series of minority pockets facing a national as well as a class problem? Within the British Labour Party had existed an affiliated minority group which had for years upheld precisely these ideas. It was called Poalei Zion, the Socialist Zionist Party. At each national convention it had resolved (and received support from the majority of the Labour Party as a whole) the establishment of a Jewish Labour Commonwealth in Palestine, and supported a Jewish National Home. Although aware of this, Laski had never been involved with the Socialist Zionists of his Party. Morris said that an executive meeting of the Poalei Zion had been convened as soon as the news of what had happened to European Jewry was verified and it was attended by Laski for the first time. He went on:

A special invitation had been issued to him with the most mixed feelings. Some bitterness existed because Laski, in the past, had ignored his Jewishness, had been indifferent to the Socialist Zionist group of the Labour Party that had long recognised the special nature of the Jewish problem and its national solution. To them, Jewish socialists like Laski had deserted their own people which was most in need of them. While only Jews would be concerned about their own people, they believed, the non-Jewish socialists of England could provide adequate leadership for the British Labour movement as a whole. Nevertheless, in this hour of emergency, it had been decided to sink differences and forget the past. Harold Laski had been sent a special invitation.

His participation was therefore, a most special event. It was more than a mere expression of solidarity. To those present it represented the return of Harold Laski, both as a socialist and as a Jew, to his people. That he was so illustrious an intellectual phenomenon in the traditions of British socialism merely embellished the event. It was not its essence. Harold Laski had come to find out the response of the Socialist Zionists of the Labour Party to the Jewish tragedy. It was to rescue every Jew who could still be got out of Hitler's Europe; it was to re-settle the survivors elsewhere after World War II ended as they could not be expected to remain amid the graveyard of their people. It was to direct their immigration to Palestine, the Jewish National Home, as only there was an entire Palestine Jewish community eager and able to absorb them and apply the therapy of a free and new-born nation. Everywhere else would be a repetition of dependence as a minority, the status of a refugee, the problem of identity. In going to Palestine they were returning home.

Morris said that there was room for both Jews and Arabs in Palestine. They could share the country as a bi-national State. If the Arabs were unwilling it would have to be partitioned into two sovereign national entities. British imperialism sought to keep both peoples in Palestine apart, and it was aided in doing so by the feudal and reactionary leaders of the Palestine Arabs who had supported Hitler during World War II. It was explained to Laski at the meeting that the Socialist Zionists were seeking brotherhood and peace with the Palestine Arab workers and a joint struggle against British imperialist rule over the country. Morris said Laski could accept this viewpoint even if it meant less than absolute justice would be accorded to the Palestine Arabs. For if the needs of both peoples had to be weighed in the balance, that of the Jews, following the Hitler experience, was the greater. He supported free Jewish immigration into the country and an attempt at a bi-national political solution.

Unfortunately, said Morris, the bi-national solution did not come about but Laski continued to support the idea long after it was apparent that, however desirable, it was impossible to achieve. He commented:

When the Labour Party came to power in Britain, after winning the first post-war general election, Clement Attlee became Prime Minister and Ernest Bevin, the Foreign Secretary. The Labour Government pursued a pro-Arab policy in Palestine and, in attempting to curtail the immigration to the country of the Jewish survivors of Europe, and the further development of the Palestine Jewish economy, it was responsible for the ensuing open and bitter clash with Zionism, led by the Socialist Zion movement. Laski, in those days, was in an impossible situation. He could not agree with the Socialist Zionists over bi-nationalism; he could agree even less with the betrayal by the Labour Government of its pre-election pledges to the Jews. As far as his own people was concerned, Harold Laski thus held a minority and untenable position in both camps. Not only in the clash between British and Zionist socialism was Harold Laski without roots or substantial backing. In the clash of forces in the British Labour Party and its Government—over British affairs—Laski was in a vulnerable position. This vulnerability has been a common denominator of socialist history. It stems from the vulnerability of the Jews as a whole outside the State of Israel.

Morris said that whilst Laski stimulated the thinking of the British Labour Party he was on the periphery of its power. This was exemplified in his clash with Ernest Bevin. Although he attained the chairmanship of the Party for a period his struggle against Bevin could only end in defeat. Morris said that both Stalin and Bevin, despite their avowed brands of socialism, were anti-Semites. Following considerable further development of the situation, Morris said that Laski, through his integrity and intellectual brilliance had rendered great service to humanity. He said that he personally, 'and many of my colleagues at the time, regretted that Harold Laski did not share with us the Israel experience. In it he might have found more intellectual and spiritual harmony'.

CHAPTER FIVE

POLITICAL THEORIST

So far in these pages we have met Laski as a student, seen him at work as a university teacher, and looked at his activities in day-to-day local and national politics. It was, of course, as a writer that he reached his widest audiences. Many of his articles and pamphlets were, understandably, of short-term interest, often concerned with current issues, but most of his books, especially those on political theory, had a longer vogue and some have a lasting value. Indeed one—*A Grammar of Politics*—which we shall look at later in this chapter, was described to me as 'a milestone on the road from Plato' by William Robson, a friend of Laski and now Emeritus Professor of Public Administration at the London School of Economics.

First of all let us look at Laski's method of putting thoughts on paper. Throughout his life he wrote all his books, pamphlets and articles by hand. He had no use at all for typewriters (and he avoided the telephone as much as he could, at home leaving his wife or daughter to deal with calls) and his handwriting had almost to be seen to be believed. He wrote a very diminutive—perhaps a better word would be 'minuscule'—hand which was not easy to read until one got quite used to it—even then it occasionally presented problems. (In one of his letters to Laski, Franklin Roosevelt, when United States President, commented: 'Ever so many thanks for that delightful note, for which, thank God, I had a large magnifying glass handy!') And only on very rare occasions did Laski make any correction or alterations whatever. As I write I have before me the original manuscript of one of his shorter books, *Introduction to Politics* (the American title is *Politics*) published in 1931. It is, of course, written in the author's characteristic handwriting and I have found only one word altered in seventy-nine very closely-written pages.

And, if he could avoid it, Laski did not write at a desk or table. He liked to use a specially-made large wooden board which he put across his knees and wrote as he sat back in a big easy chair. During one of my talks with Otto Kahn-Freund (to whom I have already referred), who was one of Laski's colleagues at the London School of Economics for some time, he confirmed the meticulous and unusual way in which he wrote. He said:

> As I talk to you now I can see Harold Laski in my mind's eye, sitting comfortably in his easy chair with his large writing-board across his knee. The first thing he always did was to draw a margin-line about an inch from the left-hand edge of the paper and then he would completely fill the page with his very small handwriting. He hardly ever seemed to alter a word but if he did feel it necessary to do so he would be likely to turn over to a clean sheet and start the page all over again. I remember an occasion, typical of many, when he was writing in the company of a number of fellow-lecturers who were carrying on a lively discussion on some current topic. Although apparently engrossed in his writing, Harold would occasionally throw in a very pertinent comment which showed very clearly that, as well as writing busily, he had been following closely all that was being said by those in the room.

Professor Graham Wootton, now of the Department of Political Science at Tuft's University in Massachusetts, told me that in his London School of Economics days he was closely associated with the Hackney Labour Party, and he asked Laski, whose student he was at the time, if he would be kind enough to write an article for a Newsletter the constituency Party was about to launch. 'Harold Laski sat down just where he was and wrote the whole article out without a moment's hesitation', Wootton told me, and he let me have sight of the manuscript which he had later taken back with him to the United States and which he had carefully preserved over the years. Here again, of course, it was written in Laski's diminutive hand, with never a word amended, and was the perfect article to inspire and encourage rank and file Party workers. 'When he had finished it', Wootton told me, 'Harold just handed the sheets to me without a word and immediately went on with what he had been writing before I made my request. On my thanking him he just said: "I hope it's what you wanted"'.

I remember an occasion when I called at Transport House to see Morgan Phillips, then General Secretary of the Labour Party, and when we had finished our business we got talking about Laski, his facility for writing, and his readiness to literally put pen to paper. Phillips recalled a day when, towards the conclusion of a committee meeting, he had been instructed, as secretary, to prepare a draft of an important pamphlet setting out Party policy. Phillips told me that he thought about it that evening, recognised it would be a formidable task, and decided to turn it over in his mind for a day or two before actually starting to write. However, when Phillips arrived at his office the following morning there was waiting for him on his desk a complete draft of the pamphlet in Laski's characteristic handwriting. It could only have meant that after the committee meeting Laski had gone home, got out pen and paper, and written the whole pamphlet before retiring for the night. 'I was astonished', Phillips told me. In a brief accompanying note Laski said that, if it was acceptable, Phillips could make use of it when settling down to do his own drafting. The Labour Party Secretary told me that he had Laski's draft immediately copied and circulated to the committee without alteration. It was readily endorsed, and in due course, printed and published. 'And when I thanked him', Phillips told me, 'all Harold said was "I'm glad if it helped"'.

Of course, it might be argued that, in the instances I have given, Laski was able to write quickly and well because he was on familiar ground but he seems to have had the same facility whatever he turned his hand to. At an hour or two's notice he would respond to an urgent editorial request for an article. I recall, and mention, just as an example, the occasion during the war when he was asked to review, for a magazine, Lord Ponsonby's biography of his father, Sir Henry Ponsonby, who was Private Secretary to Queen Victoria. John Wheeler-Bennett, the historian, thought so highly of what Laski wrote that he quoted from it very extensively in his biography of King George VI. He said it was 'entirely applicable to the office of Private Secretary in the present day'.

And, turning to Laski's books, it is felt by some that his most scholarly work was written before he was thirty-five. Indeed some consider that he never got beyond these early works and 'never fulfilled as a writer the high hopes that were aroused by his youthful brilliance'. Often referred to as 'the Big Four' they were *Problems of Sovereignty* (written in 1917 whilst he was still teaching at Harvard), *Authority in the Modern State* (1919), *The Foundations of Sovereignty* (1921) and his *magnum opus*, *A Grammar of Politics* which was published in 1925.

A Grammar of Politics (it covers nearly seven hundred closely printed pages) soon became recognised internationally as a university textbook and before long had been translated into several languages. Although it is now fifty years since it was written it is still widely used by students, and, as Laski explained, the volume completed an effort begun some years earlier 'to construct a theory of the place of the State in the great Society'. He explained that his earlier volumes were either mainly critical or intended to discuss somewhat technical issues in political philosophy. The *Grammar* (as it is familiarly and almost affectionately referred to) was more positive, since it attempted to outline the institutions which researches had suggested as desirable. And the author sought, as far as he could, to discuss the objections of those who criticised his earlier volumes.

Early in the book on sovereignty, Laski says:

That the State is, in some form or another, an inevitable organisation will be apparent to anyone who examines the human nature that we encounter in daily life. But to admit that it is inevitable is not to admit that it is entitled to moral pre-eminence of any kind. For, after all, the State is not itself an end, but merely the means to an end, which is realised only in the enrichment of human lives. Its power and the allegiance it can win depend always upon what it achieves for that enrichment. We are, that is to say, subjects of the State, not for its purpose, but for our own. Realisable good means always some happiness won for the lives of persons, or it means nothing. Power, therefore, must seek the widest possible distribution of such happiness. We are entitled to suspect the State save as we see under its aegis the unfettered growth of human personality. We are entitled to condemn it save as its powers are used deliberately to defeat the forces which stand in the way of that growth. Ultimately, at least, the minds of men can give service to no end less than the realisation of what is best in themselves. They can give allegiance to no lesser ideal. They exercise most truly their citizenship when they seek with wisdom a release from the service, alike material and spiritual, that is born of the perversion of power.

And the volume's concluding message, written at the end of a chapter which surveys the international scene, is:

> The sovereignty of the State, then, is in the process of disappearance in international affairs because it has served its purpose there. It no longer enfolds and absorbs the allegiance of the individual; his loyalties are as diverse as his experience of life. As he grows into the consciousness of the world, so does he reduce that world to the service of his personality. He is coming to see that the categories utilised by the State when it sought freedom from religious bondage are no longer valid. What he requires is not the concepts of imperialism, but the concepts of federation. What he has come to see is the futility of independence in a world which is interdependent. There are concerns where he will allow intervention from none. There are matters where with those about him of his own kindred he claims the right to self-determination. Beyond, there are the greater issues which he sees are the common concern of mankind. It is the paradox of self-government that, to be free, he must share with others in making the rules of fellowship among men. But life has taught us in the sternest fashion that without those rules there will be no fellowship, and without fellowship there will be no freedom. Either we have to make a world by deliberate plan, or we court disaster. It is a grim alternative. It make men feel how near their feet lie to the abyss. But it is also an alternative that may prove the pathway to their salvation.

It is clear that the problems of sovereignty constantly exercised Laski's mind over the years, he asking himself the question: 'Since government is necessary, who is to give orders to whom and upon what terms?' and he strove hard to find the answer. Talking to members of the Harold Laski Institute of Political Science in Ahmedabad, India, ten years after Laski's death, Gagenvihari L. Mehta (who had been a pupil of his at the London School of Economics) explained Laski's approach to the problem as he saw it like this:

> In his dissertations on sovereignty, Laski set out with a wealth of historical and legal data to show that the State was not absolute nor unitary as maintained by political philosophers and jurists. He said that society is essentially federal in nature, and that the State which is only one among many social institutions is important but not supreme. The State, in other words, is distributive, not collective: political relationship, consequently, should be functional and power decentralised. Laski held that the omnicompetence of the State was

not right in principle and was detrimental to common welfare. Even Karl Marx wanted the State to wither away. It was an abstraction when we take into account various voluntary organisations functioning in a society such as labour unions and employers' federations and farmers' associations, and several bodies of producers and consumers, which, in effect, impinge on the sphere and jurisdiction of the political State (or more simply, Government) and shared its power and influenced its decisions. He did not, however, explain how co-ordination is to be achieved between these various institutions, who should achieve it and whether the co-ordinating organisation would not be superior to the others.

Nor did Laski accept the principle of unquestioning obedience to authority enunciated by idealists and advocates of state sovereignty. He thought that the State should be judged like any other social institution in the light of its actual contribution to the well-being of its citizens. A theory of ultimate sovereignty of the State tended to establish a monolithic authority usurping the initiative which could more appropriately and usefully rest with groups and associations and with citizens developing their individuality and spontaneity. In a complex society intersected by diverse interests many of which are conflicting—producers and consumers, urban and rural populations, workers and employers, the haves and the have-nots—there is no such 'general will' as postulated in textbooks of political science. We should, Laski argued, be concrete if our conceptions and theories are to be realistic or even capable of being understood and implemented.

This thesis which Laski propounded with vigour and acumen was akin to pluralism. Its emphasis was not so much on the legal and juristic aspects of the State as on the economic and social forces which determine the content of law, mould the character of government and shape the objectives and activities of those in power. It was an endeavour to discover a philosophic base for a theory of the State which, in many ways, was bold, imaginative and realistic. It showed a marked individualist strain in his outlook; he rejected formal unity and static order because he held that the good that is to be achieved in a society is, in the ultimate analysis, the good of the individual who should be the final judge of the worth of the actions of the State. 'The only permanent safeguard of democratic government', he wrote, 'is that the unchanging and ultimate sanction of the intellectual decision should be the conscience.' It has been argued that such a theory would make for anarchy. This is not the place to deal with the implications, doctrinal and practical, of such a thesis. One point, however, must be made. Conscience in such a concept as Laski's is not caprice nor a stray impulse. It has to be an instructed moral sense, a profounder rationality which is in harmony with the whole personality of a responsible individual. Because of his insistence on the conscience of an individual citizen as the ultimate arbiter, Laski argued that there are moral limits to the sovereignty and authority of the State. And he upheld the right of disobedience where a grievous wrong is felt or the dignity of the human being is outraged.

As those familiar with Laski's writings know so well, time and again he returned over the years to the fundamental questions of the State and Government. Men and women looked to the State to make their lives worth living and it was because they often looked in vain that they wavered in their allegiance. While in *A Grammar of Politics* he made his proposition that the State is 'an organisation for enabling the mass of men to realise social good on the largest possible scale' Laski repeatedly asserted that if there is a restriction of economic power to one group, it follows that political power, too, will be found there. He said in *The State in Theory and Practice* that the true end of the State is the 'creation of those conditions under which the members of the State may attain the maximum satisfaction of their desires' and that 'any State in which the instruments of property are in private hands is, by that fact, biased in its incidence. It may state the rights it confers in universal terms; it confines their effective enjoyment to the owners of property'. And in his *The Rise of European Liberalism*, which is concerned, as he was so often, with the interdependence of economics and politics, Laski says:

For what produced liberalism was the emergence of a new economic society at the end of the middle ages. As a doctrine, it was shaped by the needs of that new society; and like all social philosophies, it could not transcend the medium in which it was born. Like all social philosophies, therefore, it contained in its birth the conditions of its own destruction. In its living principle, it was the idea by which the new middle class rose to a position of political dominance. Its instrument was the discovery of what may be called the contractual State. To make that State, it sought to limit political intervention to the narrowest area compatible with the maintenance of public order. It never understood, or was never able to fully admit, that freedom of contract is never genuinely free until the parties thereto have equal bargaining power. This, of necessity, is a function of equal material conditions.

Laski comments, after considerable development of his argument:

> It is true enough that economic liberalism lifted the chains of State-servitude from the middle class; but it is not less true that it was the necessary outcome of its acceptance that the men so freed riveted those chains upon the workers who had helped them to their freedom.

As Norman MacKenzie, whom I have previously quoted, has commented, repeatedly, Laski asked: 'How can we overcome the antithesis between individual property rights in the means of production and the fulfilment of the democratic idea; how give liberty meaning except in the context of equality; how to make men genuinely equal before the law?' MacKenzie goes on:

> The basis of Laski's socialist faith lay in his fear that democracy, born of a nascent capitalism might die at the hands of capitalism in decay, and in the rise of Fascism he found confirmation of this fear. From 1927, when his small volume on *Communism* appeared, through the Great Depression, which provoked *Democracy in Crisis* and *The State in Theory and Practice*, and through the reactionary drift of the thirties, reflected in *Parliamentary Government in England* there runs the opposing themes of pessimism and optimism. The pessimism led him to doubt whether the crisis of our times could have any other outcome than violent social conflict. The optimism sprang from his hope—on which he always acted in politics—that in Britain at least, political democracy had acquired sufficient vitality and momentum to master the crisis in peace by creating a social democracy. It is suggestive that the pessimism was most marked in his academic writings and the optimism most pronounced when he was actually called upon to make political decisions. In this context, *Revolution by Consent*, small and ephemeral though it was, seems in retrospect to be perhaps his most characteristic book. For here, in the midst of war, he made his most urgent plea for the willing and rapid liquidation of capitalism by democratic processes, but joined with this a prophesy of social catastrophe if the opportunity—it might be, he thought the last opportunity—were to be missed.

Incidentally, Laski wrote to Holmes in November 1927 to say that 'the publisher of my *Communism* has gone bankrupt with the result that instead of the £400 he owes me (it has sold some 40,000 copies) I shall have, I understand, about £10. . . . It is, I think, bad luck to have written a "best seller" and then be deprived of the fruits thereof. But I see no other way of meeting it except to shrug one's shoulders and go on to the next thing.'

Laski's *Parliamentary Government in England* is, to a considerable extent, concerned with the question as to whether the Parliamentary method can be used to transform the social foundation on which it rests and can continue after such a transformation. It was published in 1938 before, of course, the measures of the Attlee Government and the recently enacted legislation and programme of the Wilson Administration. A reviewer in *The Times* commented when the book appeared that Laski

> believes that the older parties are only loyal to the constitution in so far as it preserves the social system from which they profit. When a Socialist Government attains power as well as office, he expects to see a defection of the propertied class, directed towards making it impossible to use the forms of the constitution to bring about the changes that make up the Labour Party's avowed programme. Not only will the flight of capital become in effect an undermining of the authority of Parliament and the administration; the Civil Service, by the temper of mind belonging to the class from which its administrative grade is recruited, will be unable to co-operate wholeheartedly with its political chiefs; and even the Judges, by their professional instinct to interpret all legislation so as to allow the minimum disturbance of the common law, which is itself a convention for the defence of property, will become, though without conscious disingenuousness, an obstacle to the fulfilment of the people's will. If the Socialist administration is then driven to revolutionary measures to sustain its authority, the responsibility for the abandonment of the historic constitutional tradition will lie with the conservative side.

In the course of the book Laski looks at some of the facets of the working of Parliamentary democracy in its present form, and he is not enthusiastic about some possible reforms including Proportional Representation. He submits that if the House of Commons were to be refashioned to correspond exactly with the way the electorate voted it would not be in a position to present to the country a strong and effective administration. He considers that the party system is the mainstay of Parliamentary democracy. In 450 pages there is, as one would expect, much close argument in a book which seeks to examine in considerable detail the various elements of the Constitution.

Just before the outbreak of war in 1939 Laski set out his

reasons for accepting the basic truth of the Marxist philosophy which he developed in his writings. He said he had reached that conclusion in an essay which was included in a small volume of 'personal philosophies' of nineteen men who had distinguished themselves in a variety of fields; it was published under the title *I Believe*. Laski said that during his early days in America he had seen, more nakedly than in Europe, the significance of the struggle between capital and labour and 'how little meaning there can be in an abstract political liberty which is subdued to the control of economic plutocracy'. He said: 'I began to perceive in the difference in the average American attitude to the February and October revolutions in Russia, how profound is the influence of the property relation in shaping opinion. I came back from America convinced that liberty has no meaning save in the context of equality and I had begun to understand that equality, also, has no meaning unless the instrument of production is socially owned.' He added that up to 1920 his socialism was, above all, the outcome of a sense of the injustice of things as they were. It had not become an insight into the processes of history.

Saying that he returned to England in 1920 'hopeful that I was going to watch the slow permeation of economic relationships by the democratic principle' he went on:

> I have been driven to the conclusion that no class voluntarily abdicates from the possession of power. I have come to learn that the private ownership of the means of production makes it impossible for the democratic idea to transcend the barriers of class without the capture of the State by the working class. The experience of Russia, the advent of Fascism in central and south-eastern Europe, the attitude of the owning class in Spain and France and the United States to all serious attempts at social reform, the general strike of 1926 and the betrayal of 1931 in England, the new imperialism of Japan and Italy, have all convinced me that, in large outline, there is no answer to the philosophy of Marx. Men broadly think in terms of an experience made and unmade by their class position.

Tracing further the events that had led him to these conclusions, Laski said in the essay that what had happened, including the failure of the League of Nations and the rise of Fascism, ruled out the Fabian method of gradualism. That principle, in his view, was the natural method to recommend in an age of capitalist expansion. In a period of capitalism's decline its result would be to give the owning class a supreme opportunity for counter-attack. He said he was convinced that 'the time has come for a central attack on the structure of capitalism. Nothing less than wholesale socialisation can remedy the position'.

People close to Laski in his later years have told me that they sensed that one of his increasing anxieties, as expressed in his writings and speeches, was that the price that would have to be paid for change by revolution was too great to contemplate. It was his fervent hope that the Western world would move to a form of socialism non-violently and without the sacrifice of individual liberty. In 1948 when the Attlee Government had been in power for three years, and had extended the welfare state and nationalised some basic industries, Laski wrote: 'We are permitted by the mental climate of this country to hope—we cannot say more than hope—for success in our effort to build a socialist Britain by democratic means.' In 1950, less than a month before he died, praising the Labour Party as the greatest Socialist Party in Europe, he wrote that it rejected 'the Marxian theory of a community which can only be made socialist by a revolution to establish the dictatorship of the proletariat, which then, by repressing all opposition, passes into a classless society'. If Laski were alive today it is interesting to speculate if he would consider the further socialist measures that have been introduced by the Wilson Government were the continued successful use of democratic methods to change still further the basis of society and the class structure. Laski was never afraid in his writings and speaking to let it be seen that he had adjusted his thinking in the light of his own experiences and events at home and abroad. As Professor Julius Lewin, formerly of Witwatersrand University in Johannesburg, put it to me: 'A good student—and Laski remained a student, using the word in its broadest sense—is ever ready to revise his opinions in the light of changing circumstances and that is exactly what he did.'

Even as a young man, whilst paying tribute to Marx's earnestness of purpose, Laski had been critical of some of his conclusions as to the inevitability and necessity for violent revolution. He wrote that he felt that what had happened in Russia emphasised that violent means to get rid of existing institutions 'entails the suppression of tolerance and kindliness, sows cruelty and hatred, anger and suspicion into the soil of human relations, has impaired at every point the intellectual heritage of the Russian people and has been impatient of reason and fanatically hostile to critical inquiry'. And in his essay 'Marx' Laski had asserted:

> That wrong can be wiped out with wrong, that we are to regard ourselves as the victims of blind and impersonal forces against which it is useless to strive, that the possessive impulses of man cannot be transcended by creative effort—these and things like these are a gospel of impossible despair. In that aspect, surely, the older socialists were right who made the basis of their creed a doctrine of right and fraternity and justice. For right and fraternity and justice imply love as their foundation; they do not spring, even at the last vain striving, for a doctrine founded upon hate.

In 1933, with the growth of Fascism in Europe and the events of 1931 in Britain still fresh in his mind, Laski had written in his *Democracy in Crisis*:

> Men who ignore the tragedies of the past have only themselves to blame if thereby they make the tragedies of the future. For revolution, like war, is infinite tragedy since, in its very nature, it means pain and suffering and the tragic confusion of means with ends. The innocent not less than the guilty are its victims. It is the enemy of Reason and Freedom—the twin goddesses whose triumph gives what of beauty there is in the ultimate texture of men's lives. Where there is social conflict, there also Hate and Fear rule the destinies of us all; and even if there is a high purpose in the price they exact, it is a purpose stained by bloody sacrifice. That is the prospect, grim and bitter and evil, we confront at the eleventh hour of what we might have made a great civilisation.

And it was at the height of the last war that Laski wrote two books on the theme that a world revolution was taking place and that whilst Russia had achieved one form of socialism the Western world should also progress towards another type, non-violently if at all possible, and without loss of the liberty of the individual. They were *Reflections on the Revolution of Our Time*, written in 1943, and *Faith, Reason and Civilisation* published a year later. Laski's championing in the latter book of revolution by consent and advocating co-operation between socialists in the West and Communists in the East was vigorously condemned in 1946 by Alexandrov, who was at that time in charge of Communist Party propaganda in the Soviet Union. He was particularly criticised for supporting co-operation but not fusion with Communists. There were references in the criticism to 'professors in bourgeois society who sell learning to serve the interests of Capital and who are ready to utter the most improbable nonsense and unconscionable stupidities and rubbish'. Laski was denounced in *Pravda* as 'one of the most active participants in the field of anti-Soviet propaganda who specialises mainly in proving the advantages of bourgeois democracy over Soviet Socialist democracy'. By advising socialists in Europe to co-operate with but never merge with Communists he was charged with 'opposing the interests of the working class'.

When *Reflections on the Revolution of our Time* was published, *The Times* newspaper reviewer commented that it was a scintillating book, and went on: 'It is not to everybody's political and economic taste but everybody will be the better for having read and—still more—having digested it. With all the intellectual clarity, erudition, moral fervour and dignified English which mark his writings, Professor Laski addressed himself to how and why Fascism rose, the causes underlying this war and the last, the crisis before which civilisation stands, and the course which mankind must set if victory is not to prove a mockery and the forces of evil and retrogression which led Germany and Italy to choose war are not to appear in other forms in other lands, not excluding this country and the United States.'

When the book appeared men's minds were turning to the kind of peace that would follow the end of the war, and Laski expresses the anxiety that, when peace does come, the opportunity might be lost to bring about fundamental changes which he considered were necessary in the structure and spirit of society. He emphasised, as he was doing in other writings and on platforms at that time, his lack of confidence in the Churchill Government to embark on what he calls the 'great reforms' that were needed. And the same uncertainty was extended to those in authority in the United States. Laski made it clear that he desperately feared that the mood which would follow victory would pass and a wonderful opportunity for fundamental changes would be lost. Looking forward, as he saw the position, 'the middle class must co-operate with the workers in essential revision, as the aristocracy was wise enough to do, even if at the eleventh hour, a century ago over the Reform Bill, or violent revolution will be unleashed by means that may well transform the ends either party to the conflict has in view'.

Faith, Reason and Civilisation was written at a time when the author was full of admiration for the Russian stand at Stalingrad and, whilst not given the same general welcome as *Reflections on the Revolution of our Time*, it was acknowledged as an essay in historical analysis that would well repay study. Laski, in developing his theme, claimed that just as in the early days of Christianity inspiration filled a need and gave people a faith and inspiration by which to live, Russian Communism had done much the same and had created a new climate of hope. It was, in his view, for the people themselves to reshape their own lives and work out their own salvation with a new set of social values.

In this book Laski advanced an argument which was a justification for his own involvement in the day-to-day world of politics. He said he felt it was the duty of intellectuals to give a lead in interpreting events and guiding the mass of people as to the road on which they should travel. After drawing examples of other days to support his contention, he said it was the failure of the Italian intellectuals that allowed Mussolini to steal power. 'It was the failure of the German intellectuals which permitted Hitler to establish his ugly empire. It was the failure of the French intellectuals, after 1919, which created conditions out of which France was overthrown in 1940. Let us not deceive ourselves into the belief that the conditions in Britain and the United States are different.'

In his book *Communism* Laski had, in 1927, said that whatever the shortcomings of Marxism it was 'far more important to grasp the truth it emphasises than to be merely denunciatory of the methods by which it seeks its ends' and in 1948, when the national executive of the Labour Party decided to celebrate the centenary of the '*Communist Manifesto*' by the publication of a new edition with a historical introduction and illustrative material, Laski was commissioned to undertake the task. He wrote an introduction occupying more than half the volume and, claiming that Marx's desire for justice for the mass of people was one of the main driving forces of his life, Laski summed it up as:

the desire to take from the shoulders of the people the burden by which it is oppressed. . . . He transformed the fears of the workers into hope, he translated their efforts from interest in political mechanisms to interest in social foundations. . . . He was often wrong, he was rarely generous, he was always bitter; yet when the roll of those to whom the emancipation of the people is due comes to be called, few will have a more honourable, and none a more eminent role.

I have already referred, in the previous chapter, to two books Laski wrote about America and to *Trade Unions in the New Society* which contains the lectures Laski gave in the United States in 1949 at the request of the foundation established to commemorate the American trade union leader Sidney Hillman. The book (which was not published in Britain until after Laski's death) was welcomed as a contribution to a subject at that time 'still too much neglected by British writers'. Laski did not try to survey the American trade union scene or deal with structure and policy but took as his theme the larger problem presented by the relations between organised Labour with the State and the attitude of Governments to it. Laski was in the fortunate position of being able to draw on his own first-hand experience of the political and industrial scene in both countries and uses the history of trade unionism in each country in turn to throw light on the issues confronting it in the other. Although fully aware of the difficulties there are in the way of forming third political parties in the United States, his assessment of the developing scene leads to the assumption by trade unions of a more positive role than in the past rather than auctioning their support to the least undesirable candidates. Laski knew of the obstacles impeding the formation of new parties in the United States and that the result of efforts made to create any new political force had been to encourage—temporarily at least—the existing parties to broaden their outlook and revise their programmes.

In a chapter entitled 'Trade Unions and Democracy' he says:

The purpose of trade unionism can never be war on the economic battlefield alone. At every critical point the struggle moves on to the political stage . . . I am therefore led to the view that the trade union movement, in a revolutionary age like our own, has a political task at least of equal importance to its economic function. No doubt it must seek, with all its power, to increase productivity; there is no other permanent way to advance the standard of life. No doubt, also, it is folly beyond defence to make demands anywhere in the realm of wages and hours, or in similar spheres, which can have no other outcome but to make inflation inevitable. It is one of the supreme duties of trade union leadership to prevent what would be a catastrophic blow to the workers' hopes, since an uncontrolled inflation usually is paid for by working class suffering.

Laski goes on to say that 'one of the most complex trade union problems of the present age and one whose solution is by no means an easy one' is the problem of the activities of the Communist Party. After referring to the position on the continent as it was at that time he says:

But in Great Britain and in the United States the situation is very different. In the former the Communists are a very small minority; out of over eight million trade unionists there are not more than fifty thousand Communist Party members at the outside; whilst in the United States I do not think the proportion is even as high. Yet there is no doubt of their influence. You may dislike the methods by which they acquire it. You may feel anger at the volume of intrigue, misrepresentations and downright lying, above all, the smear tactics they do not hesitate to use. Yet, when the last criticism has been made of the Communists, I think it urgent to recognise that by far the largest part of their influence is due to their great zeal, the continuity of their devotion to the purposes they seek to serve, and the faith they have in the over-all end to which they give so intense a devotion. At a branch meeting their record of attendance far surpasses that of non-communists. If there is a long, sometimes tiresome agenda they can be relied upon to endure it when others, wearied by the fatigue of endless petty detail decide to go home. If there is an election of an official they do not bring forward half a dozen candidates; they are careful to arrange their candidates so that the maximum votes for which they can hope are concentrated on a single person. They do not leave their members to find their way about trade union work by the light of nature. The communist in a trade union is not only the recipient of instructions, he must carry out; he is carefully trained in the art of how best to carry out instructions. He knows that where grievance exists his business is to take the lead in exploiting it. He is constantly on the alert for the chance to discuss, to analyse, to explain. Where difficulties emerge reaching beyond the factory or mine where he works he is not only told in detail the policy he must follow but he becomes as it were, the liaison officer in a line of contacts, each member of which is urging the same policy in the same way.

In a chapter concerned with Laski's output of the written word reference must be made to the Holmes–Laski letters which, as I said in the chapter on Laski's early days in America, were a direct outcome of a meeting in 1916 between Laski and Justice Holmes, one a young man of twenty-three and the other a judge of the United States Supreme Court in his seventies. They corresponded almost weekly for nearly twenty years—until Holmes died—and their letters were published in two large volumes of 1,400 pages by the Harvard University Press three years after Laski's death. The two writers, in addition to commenting on personal and family matters (just a few of which I have quoted in these pages) exchanged views on history, political theory, law and literature. Although politically they were poles apart, as has been said 'it is a tribute to the civilised intellectual endowment of both that the wide differences between them never move to any departure from the high level of intellectual and affectionate regard and respect'.

Although they respected each other's views they never had any qualms about making known their disagreement. In one letter to Holmes, Laski wrote: 'Your letter was indeed a delight; and though I should, I think, deny almost the whole of your economic diagnosis as born of a philosophy contradicted by the whole trend of modern fact and analysis, I enjoyed every word of it. I add that it is at bottom the economics of the soldier who accepts a rough equation between "isness" and "oughtness". I see no validity in such a creed except upon principles I would deny at the stake.' And a typical Holmes comment was: 'I haven't quite finished your book. You state the pros and cons fairly but with an implied sympathy for beliefs that I believe to be noxious humbugs that grieves me.'

There have been references, in comment on the letters, to 'the delight of letting free minds roam widely and deeply over the broadest range of human knowledge and thought' and the mutual friend who brought Holmes and Laski together, Felix Frankfurter, spoke of the letters as the 'interplay of two such untrammelled adventurers of the spirit'. An American commentator has said that 'for any who would refrain from sampling because of hostility to views and causes which are here espoused by one friend or the other, one can only suggest that the deep divergence did not deprive them of serene and thrilling joy in sharing with each other their minds and hearts'. When she learned I was writing this book Mrs Laski very kindly gave me a copy of the letters but I am afraid that in this volume it is impracticable to quote adequately from the 750,000 words that the two correspondents exchanged, all in their own handwriting.

When Laski died he was writing a new book *The Dilemma of Our Times* which was issued in 1952 by his literary executors. The dilemma which concerned him during the last few years of his life, and about which he felt he must write, arose out of the failure of the Soviet Union to justify the optimism of those who, during the war, had anticipated that when peace came there would be a new world dominated by the major powers working together. Bitterly disappointed by Molotov's refusal even to discuss the Marshall Plan he said that Russian policy 'had the ugly look of a conscious effort to block the hope of that recovery by splitting the European continent into two camps'. Arguing that both the Western powers and the Soviet Union were responsible for the cold war, he wrote:

I do not think anything is to be gained by the attempt to measure the degree of responsibility for its inception which all the great Powers have incurred; it is as foolish to blame Russian Communism and its devotees in other countries for the cleavage from which we suffer as it is to insist that America and Great Britain are seeking by different ways to arrest, and, ultimately to destroy, the communist idea in the interest of the privileged classes which are fighting to retain their traditional authority.

And he goes on to claim that, just as those in power in the Soviet Union condemn anyone who questions Russian policy, so 'the rulers of the United States are driven by a wild hysteria to denounce and to persecute those among their citizens who think that there may be something of social import in the dogmas to which Soviet Russia pins its faith'. But he says it would be absurd to suggest that 'witch-hunting' in America had even begun to be on anywhere near the scale it is practised in Russia.

It would seem that as time had gone on since the advent of a Labour Government in 1945, Laski had become increasingly pessimistic about the likelihood of a more intimate relationship between this country and the Soviet Union. He referred to the Communists' continued criticism of British Labour and its policies and commented: 'So far from the advance of socialism in Great Britain having assisted closer Anglo-Russian relations, it seems, as far as Moscow is concerned, to have assisted in their deterioration.' He felt that Britain should steer clear of alliance with either Moscow or Washington and should follow an independent foreign policy.

Whilst at the time of their publication reviewers and political commentators devoted considerable space to what Laski had to say in his books, and there was much favourable comment, there were sometimes reservations about his style of writing as well as about what he had to say. And it should not be thought that uncertainties were expressed only by those who disagreed with what Laski wrote. His close friend for many years, Kingsley Martin, said that 'in his passionate desire to persuade his generation of the danger in which society stood he wrote too much and repeated himself too often and neglected those periods of lonely thought out of which creative ideas spring'. He added: 'Sometimes one feels that Laski was the most verbose and redundant of writers and that a quarter of the words could have been advantageously deleted. At other times one is impressed by the constant brilliance of phrase and an epigrammatic quality which are rare in political writing.'

There is no doubt that some of what Laski wrote continues to exercise men's minds, and it is interesting to note that as recently as mid-1974 George Feaver, of the Department of Political Science at the University of British Columbia, gave an address 'Intellectuals and Politics: Harold Laski Revisited' to the Canadian Political Science Association at the University of Toronto. I had a talk with him about the occasion recently and he said he was most impressed with the enthusiasm of his listeners. In Feaver's address there was, as one would expect, substantial quotations from Laski's writings and a review of the developments in his thinking over the years. At the end of his address Feaver quoted Max Beloff's reference, in the June 1950 *Fortnightly Review*, to his generation as 'The Age of Laski'.

I have only been able in this chapter to refer to some of the score of books that Laski wrote in addition to a large number of pamphlets and innumerable articles for journals and newspapers. We have, however, been able to see something of the process by which he reached his political convictions. It has not been my intention to try to write a treatise on Laski as a political thinker but rather to give a picture of the whole man as he grew up and was known to people all over the world who came under his influence, shared his interests and enjoyed his companionship.

For years before he died Laski had been very busy collecting material with a view to one day writing a comprehensive study of European political thought. He had, as occasion permitted, carried out considerable research and made extensive notes to that end. He had collected, in his private library, copies of many rare publications (especially French political books of the sixteenth and seventeenth centuries) to help him to achieve that on which he had set his heart. It was a unique collection of material of which he was very proud and he was known to be looking forward to the day when, at least partially retired from politics, he could settle down quietly to write. Alas it was not to be!

CHAPTER SIX

CHAIRMAN OF THE LABOUR PARTY

During the war Laski became more and more convinced that Clement Attlee should relinquish the leadership of the Parliamentary Labour Party. He had succeeded George Lansbury just before the 1935 General Election and was now a member of the War Cabinet and Deputy Prime Minister to Winston Churchill in the Coalition Government.

Laski, looking towards the end of hostilities and the General Election that would doubtless follow, felt that Attlee did not have the qualities to lead the Labour Party to electoral victory and he never hesitated to make his view known both at home and abroad, to the embarrassment of his political associates. In 1943, for instance, the Party's national executive committee gave consideration to an article which Laski had contributed to a number of American publications in which he said that to cling to Attlee in the next election would mean defeat. Attlee, Laski wrote, only retained his place because the Party could not make up its mind between Ernest Bevin and Herbert Morrison. After a tribute to Attlee's integrity he spoke of him as uninspiring and uninteresting. The executive, in a statement issued at the conclusion of its meeting, said that Laski was a member of the national executive and the committee wished to make it clear that it disassociated itself from the statements made in the articles.

Whilst writing this book I talked about Laski's attitude to Attlee's leadership with Philip Noel-Baker, Labour MP for well over thirty years and a member of both Ramsay MacDonald's and Attlee's Governments. He told me that Laski was not alone amongst Labour MPs in the late 1930s and early 1940s in having doubts about Attlee's suitability to lead the Party especially if it should attain power. 'There was, from time to time, talk of him being replaced by Morrison', Noel-Baker told me, 'but nothing came of it and we all know that, in the event, Clement Attlee made a very good Prime Minister.'

During the early war years Laski acted as Attlee's personal assistant but it does not seem to have been a very auspicious partnership and just a year before the end of the war in Europe Laski wrote critically to Attlee in the course of which he used the word 'MacDonaldism' a reference to the feeling in the Labour Party that, in the 1931 crisis, Ramsay MacDonald, then Labour Prime Minister, had betrayed his Party and defected to his political opponents. In the course of a very long reply, in which he reviewed both the then current and likely post-war problems, Attlee ended by saying: '... I am sorry you suggest I am verging towards MacDonaldism. As you have so well pointed out I have neither the personality nor the distinction to tempt me to think I should have any value apart from the Party I serve. I hope you will also believe that because I am face to face with practical problems I am none the less firm in the Socialist faith and that I have not the slightest desire to depart from it.'

The 1945 annual conference of the Labour Party was held at Blackpool in mid-May amidst considerable excitement. The war in Europe had just ended victoriously and during that week Prime Minister Churchill took action which brought the wartime Coalition Government to an end and he became head of a brief Conservative 'caretaker' Government. He had rejected a plea by the Labour members of the War Cabinet that the election should be postponed until October (when a new electoral register would be available, replacing the current one which was very out of date) and had decided on an early election to be held on 5 July. This momentous development gave increased impetus to those who wanted the Labour Party to have a new leader ready for the election and there was some lobbying during the week at Blackpool. The conference chairman Ellen Wilkinson (MP for Jarrow whom Attlee later selected as Minister of Education) and Laski were openly campaigning for Attlee's replacement by Morrison who, years later, wrote in his autobiography: 'I was disturbed to learn that moves had begun to propose me as leader in place of Attlee. I promptly took steps to see that these activities stopped.' One can only say that in the light of subsequent events

—and remembering that Morrison was a candidate for the leadership and how bitterly disappointed he was when Attlee was selected—this is very hard to accept.

At the conclusion of the conference Laski was chosen as chairman of the Party's national executive committee for the next twelve months—as a senior member of the executive in terms of service on the committee—and this carried with it the title of Chairman of the Labour Party.

Laski did not resort to intriguing behind Attlee's back but continued to advocate openly what he had in mind, and shortly after his return from the Blackpool conference he sent Attlee a long letter (in his own very diminutive handwriting) which is before me as I write. I am reproducing it in full because it is an indication of the strength of Laski's feeling. He wrote:

My Dear Clem,

This is a very difficult letter to write, as it involves the hard work of reconciling private regard with public obligation. But you and I have known one another, I hope, for enough time for you to recognise that I have no motive save public duty in writing to you.

I have been acutely aware for many months but especially during the Blackpool conference of the strong feeling that the continuance of your leadership in the Party is a grave handicap to our hopes of victory in the coming election. This is a wide feeling. It is felt by a majority of our own executive. It is felt by the outstanding trade union leaders. It is felt by many of the candidates, not least by the very able young service candidates who made the conference so notable. And the rank and file, whether agents or ordinary delegates who give their aid voluntarily to the Party share this view profoundly. So, as I found, do many of your Parliamentary colleagues, above all, the colleagues who are most active in the House of Commons. This discontent has reached the point of procedural discussions about a new and immediate test of the opinion of the Parliamentary Party in order to enable the campaign to have a new leader.

No one, to my knowledge, has anything but respect for your character and high integrity. No one but admits your real power as a committee-man and your devotion to the movement. It is agreed universally that you have worked with generous unselfishness for our whole nation as Deputy Prime Minister. But it is not less strongly agreed that the peculiar personal qualities which the leader of the Party now requires, the sense of the dramatic, the power to give a lead, the ability to reach the masses, the maintenance of an intimate relation with your immediate followers, the definition of great issues in a great way,—that these require a different personality from yours.

As chairman of the Party at this critical moment, not only in the history of the movement but also in the history of the nation, I should be failing in my obligations if I did not set these considerations before you and ask you, regretfully, but with a grave sense of my responsibility to draw from them the inference that your resignation of the leadership now would be a great service to the Party, just as Mr Churchill changed Auckinleck for Montgomery before El Alamein. So I suggest you owe it to the Party to give it the chance of making a comparable change on the eve of this greatest of our battles.

I need not remind you that this is not a new situation in the history of a party. Lord John Russell had to give way to Palmerston, Stafford Northcote to Randolph Churchill, Arthur Balfour to Bonar Law, Asquith to Lloyd George, Chamberlain to Winston Churchill, because each, with all his qualities, lacked just those attributes which the hour required when the change was made. I suggest, with very great respect, that this is true in your case today; that your greatest service to the Party at this moment would be an immediate self-denying ordinance of your right to the first place. Everyone in the Party wants you as a colleague high in its councils; everyone, too, knows that you have a distinguished contribution to make to its future. But I think, in all sincerity, that it would be widely and profoundly felt that a change from your leadership now would add greatly to our chance of victory. The Parliamentary Party could then, next week, exercise its prerogative of choosing a new leader to take us into the campaign.

This has been a hard letter to write; I fear it may be a painful letter for you to read. Please believe that I would not have dreamed of writing it had I not heard and weighed the profound evidence of the conviction that the situation does not admit of delay. Personal friendships and convenience would have prompted me to remain silent. But, at this level of public duty, I feel, as I am quite sure you will feel, that silence would be an indefensible betrayal of my duty. I hope, therefore, that you will read this letter in the same spirit as I have written it,—the desire to prepare the Party for action upon which, it is not improbable, the future of Parliamentary Democracy may largely depend. I am convinced that you are selfless and single-minded enough to put the Party's cause first and yourself second, in your reflection on the grave issues we have to face.

Yours ever, Harold J. Laski

Attlee took no notice of that letter and the result of the 1945

General Election is now, of course, a matter of history, Attlee leading his Party to an overwhelming victory. The declaration of the poll in the constituencies was deferred for three weeks (because of holidays in the north of England and to gather in the service votes) and it was on 26 July that the country learned that Labour had won 393 seats, the Conservatives 213, the Liberals 12 and 'others' 22.

During the afternoon of that day Laski continued his efforts to persuade Attlee—should Churchill concede defeat and decide to tender immediately his resignation to the King—not to accept an invitation to go to the Palace but to wait a day or two later until there had been a meeting of the newly-elected Parliamentary Labour Party and they had been given a chance to elect a leader. He sent an urgent letter to Attlee in which he stressed that under the constitution of the Parliamentary Labour Party the leader was elected at the beginning of each session and that Attlee should refuse to form a Government until the new MPs had met and made their choice. Attlee's reply was: 'Dear Laski: I thank you for your letter, the contents of which have been noted.' Amongst other moves was one by Morrison whose tactics included his expressing to Attlee a reluctance to serve under him as he thought the Party might want him as Prime Minister. Laski also tried to persuade Arthur Deakin (Bevin's successor as General Secretary of the Transport and General Workers' Union) to go to Bevin and ask him to be the leader with Morrison as his deputy. When Bevin heard what was going on he was furious. He said to Deakin, 'How dare you talk to me like this' and having heard that Morrison had approached Attlee he phoned Morrison and said: 'If you go on mucking about like this you won't be in the bloody Government at all.' In addition to having a high personal regard for Attlee, whom he trusted completely, Bevin considered that Attlee was the only man who could hope to keep control in the Cabinet of such widely-differing personalities. There was, too, the conviction that he had led the Party with great skill during the campaign and that the electorate believed that, when they voted Labour, Attlee was the man they were sending to Downing Street.

That evening there was a great Victory Rally at the Central Hall, Westminster, just across the road from the Houses of Parliament. I was there that night and I remember seeing

Morrison in a most jubilant mood at the outset of the meeting. It is on record that he said to two colleagues: 'There is a chance I shall be offered the premiership. I am not sure I am big enough for it. What do you think?' and, to a newly-elected MP: 'We cannot have this man as our leader.' However, during the evening the issue was put beyond doubt. Whilst the speeches were going on Attlee came into the crowded hall quietly by the side of the platform almost unnoticed. Later, towards the end of an obviously unprepared speech he said: 'I ask from you all the support we shall need to carry us triumphantly through the difficult years to the great era which is opening before us' and then, almost casually, he added that he had come to the rally straight from Buckingham Palace where he had, as he put it 'accepted His Majesty's commission to form a Government'. I recall Mrs Attlee (who had driven her husband to the Palace in their car and waited outside in the forecourt whilst he had an audience with the King) smiling broadly as the packed audience cheered wildly. This announcement must have come as a surprise to Laski who as chairman had introduced Attlee to the meeting as the 'leader of the Labour Party'. However, he immediately jumped up and enthusiastically congratulated Attlee on his 'assumption of office'.

What had happened was that Attlee had received a letter from Churchill in the middle of the afternoon conceding the election, congratulating him and saying that he would shortly be going to the Palace to resign and recommend Attlee as his successor. Attlee felt that in accepting the invitation to go to the Palace, which came in the early evening when he was having tea with his family at the Great Western Hotel, Paddington, he was acting correctly on constitutional grounds as well as having historical precedent on his side. He put it this way: 'If invited by the King to form a Government you do not say you can't reply for forty-eight hours. You accept the commission and you either bring it off successfully or you don't, and if you don't you go back and say you can't and advise the King to send for someone else.'

It will have been seen that through all these exchanges Attlee maintained his imperturbability and at a meeting of the newly-elected Parliamentary Labour Party on 28 July at Beaver Hall in the city he was given a standing ovation lasting several minutes and unanimously re-elected as leader. When forming his Cabinet he showed that he fully recognised Morrison's long experience and claim to high office by making him Lord President of the Council (a kind of overlord on the home front) and Leader of the House of Commons. The strained relationship between Bevin and Morrison was, it is believed, one of the reasons that prompted Attlee to change his mind when forming his Cabinet. He had originally intended that Hugh Dalton should be Foreign Secretary and Bevin, Chancellor of the Exchequer (a job he wanted) but later decided against this. He gave Dalton the Treasury and Bevin the Foreign Office thus keeping him apart from Morrison, one on the home front and the other mainly concerned with affairs abroad. And the incident did not assist the relationship between Bevin and Laski whom he spoke of as an 'intellectual' with all that he intended the word should imply. Things got even worse later, mainly as a result of Laski's comments on Bevin's foreign policy particularly with reference to Palestine. Bevin got to the stage when he would have nothing at all to do with him, which Laski put down to the Foreign Secretary's anti-semitism.

It is an interesting sidelight on Attlee's character that, when writing his autobiography, he devoted only one sentence to this episode of his career. It reads: 'Laski, incidentally, had tried very hard to substitute Morrison for me as Leader of the Party in the General Election but failed to get any response.' I had the privilege of helping Attlee when he was writing his memoirs and, as you would expect, got to know him rather well. During one of the long talks we had I suggested that he ought to explain the circumstances of the Laski intervention at least a little more fully. He was always ready to consider, and very often adopt, suggestions I made, but on this occasion all he said was: 'I'd rather leave it at that; I'd prefer to let it rest there.'

During the election campaign Laski's name was never missing from newspaper headlines for long. An example that readily comes to mind is when he issued a statement concerning Prime Minister Churchill's invitation to Attlee to accompany him to a forthcoming meeting at Potsdam of Marshal Stalin, President Truman and himself. Even before Churchill had time to send Attlee an official invitation (he had made his intention known to Parliament) Laski had said, in a statement to the Press:

> It is of course essential that if Mr Attlee attends this gathering he shall do so in the role of an observer only. Obviously it is desirable that the leader of the Party which may shortly be elected to govern

the country should know what is said, discussed and agreed at this vitally important meeting. On the other hand, the Labour Party cannot be committed to any decisions arrived at for the three Powers will be discussing matters which have not been debated either in the Party executive or at meetings of the Parliamentary Labour Party. Labour has a foreign policy which in many respects will not be continuous with that of a Tory-dominated coalition. It has, in fact, a far sounder foreign policy. It is therefore essential that, though Mr Attlee should attend the Three Power Talks, Labour and he should not accept responsibility for agreements which on the British side will have been concluded by Mr Churchill as Prime Minister. It is essential also that Mr Churchill himself, Marshal Stalin and President Truman should be fully aware of the position.

Laski also sent a letter to Attlee (of which nothing came) along the lines of his Press statement, adding: 'If you do not share my view I think I must, as chairman, call a special meeting of the executive committee to consider the point. This is far too grave a matter to settle without discussion if expectation of acceptance is implied in your presence with the Prime Minister.'

The day following Laski's widely-publicised statement Churchill wrote to Attlee:

I now send you a formal invitation to come with us to the forthcoming tripartite conference in the near future. Since I announced this intention to Parliament I observe that a statement was made last night by Professor Harold Laski, the chairman of the Labour Party, in which he said: 'It is, of course, essential that if Mr Attlee attends this gathering he shall do so in the role of observer only.'

His Majesty's Government must of course, bear the responsibility for all decisions. But my idea was that you should come as a friend and counsellor and help us on all the subjects on which we have been so long agreed, and have been known to be agreed by public declaration. In practice, I thought the British delegation would work just as they did at San Francisco, except that, as I have already stated, you would not have official responsibility to the Crown otherwise than as a Privy Councillor.

Merely to come as a mute observer would, I think, be derogatory to your position as the leader of your Party, and I should not have a right to throw this burden upon you in such circumstances. I hope, however, I may have your assurance that you accept my invitation.

Attlee, following Churchill's policy of sending copies of his letters to the Press, wasted no time in replying:

I thank you for your letter of today's date. I had already, on your informal intimation to me of your intention to invite me as the leader of the Labour Party to accompany you to the prospective conference in Berlin, consulted my principal colleagues in the House of Commons. They agreed with me that the offer should be accepted on the basis you have set out in your letter.

There never was any suggestion that I should go as a mere observer. I have therefore the pleasure of accepting your invitation.

There seems to me to be great public advantage in preserving and presenting to the world at this time that unity on foreign policy which we maintained throughout the last five years. I do not anticipate that we shall differ on the main lines of policy which we have discussed together so often.

I understand, of course, that responsibility must rest with the Government but I take it that we should consult together upon the issues that arise in order to present a policy consonant with the views of the great majority of the people of this country. The parallels which you draw to the arrangements at San Francisco (when the United Nations was founded) are, I think, apposite.

I appreciate that you have made this offer in view of the special conditions existing at the present time, and that I should not base any claims to a precedent on the fact of its having been made.

Laski had followed this exchange of letters with a statement that: 'Everything has now been satisfactorily cleared up. Mr Churchill had not made the position quite clear in the House of Commons. But now, with the exchange of letters, and now that the responsibility has been defined, the position is entirely satisfactory.'

A couple of days before the nation went to the polls Churchill had initiated a further lengthy correspondence with Attlee (copies of which he sent to the Press) raising the question of the authority of the national executive committee of the Labour Party. He quoted from speeches which Laski had continued to make in the country and the exchange of letters was rounded off by Attlee telling Churchill that the relative positions of the Party's executive committee and the Parliamentary Labour Party remained as always and that 'the new position with which we are confronted exists only in your own mind'. He added 'the chairman (of the executive committee of the Labour Party) has not the power to give me instructions nor do his remarks to a Press correspondent constitute the official authoritative and reiterated instructions of the executive committee of the Labour Party'. After quoting from the Party's constitution which provided for consultation between the national executive committee and the Parliamentary Labour Party Attlee went on: 'For instance, when I decided to advise the Labour Party to support you in forming an all-party Government in 1940 I consulted the executive committee before bringing it before the annual conference of the Party then in session. You raised no constitutional objection then; indeed you were glad to have the backing of this democratically elected conference. At no time, and in no circumstances, has the national executive committee ever sought to give or given instructions to the Parliamentary Labour Party arising out of the consultations. Indeed, as will be seen from the clause it has no power to do so.'

Right to the very end of the election campaign Conservative speakers and newspapers supporting their cause continued to use Laski as a 'bogey-man'. To give an example, Lord Beaverbrook, speaking at Streatham Baths in support of the Conservative candidate said: 'Professor Laski is the chairman of the Labour Party executive. He is the head of the Socialist caucus. It is commonly known as the national executive. Now this caucus has some secret protocols. Laski has made it clear that it has a foreign policy which it means to force on the House of Commons but it is a secret policy. Laski will not tell us what the national executive will do if the Socialists come to power. He will not tell us what changes he will make in the foreign policy of Churchill and Eden.'

Beaverbrook then read out the names of the Labour Party executive and added: 'You will see that this list is made up largely of men who are not in Parliament. These are the men who will deprive Parliament of its constitutional duty of discussing and disposing of the foreign affairs of this country, if Laski had his way. Britain's foreign policy will be decided not by the elected representatives of the people but by the 25 members of the national executive. In fact, the simple issue at this election is: shall foreign policy be decided by the House of Commons or by the Laski council? I hereby declare that Laski is aiming at the destruction of the Parliamentary system in Great Britain and that he hopes to set up in its place the dictatorship of something commonly called the National Executive.'

When Churchill said in a nation-wide radio broadcast that if Labour got power it would have 'to fall back on some kind of

Gestapo' Beaverbrook's *Daily Express* declared 'Call them *National* Socialists' and alleged that Labour leaders wanted to bypass Parliament 'by exactly the method used by Hitler to turn the Reichstag into a mockery'. Just before polling day the *Express*'s sister paper, the London *Evening Standard* reproduced photographs of Laski and the other members of the Labour Party executive with the caption: 'These People want to be Dictators. *Study their faces.*'

There was much speculation at the time as to why Churchill used the language he did during that broadcast right at the outset of the election campaign. He spoke of Labour's policy as 'an attack not only upon British enterprise but upon the right of an ordinary man or woman to breathe freely without having a harsh, tyrannical hand clapped across their mouths and nostrils'. Harold Macmillan (who lost his seat at Stockton-on-Tees) said in his memoirs that Churchill had been impressed by statements made by Laski but that the use of the 'terrible word' Gestapo was a grievous error. He thought Churchill's speech was a 'turning point to our disadvantage' and that it was 'easy to deride as an outrage the implied attack on colleagues with whom he had been working in perfect amity for the last five years,—men of moderate opinions such as Attlee, Morrison and, above all, Bevin'.

Right up to polling day newspaper reporters followed Laski wherever he went and in a speech at Coggeshall in Essex he asked the audience not to think that he was under any delusions about his position. He said that at every election since 1918 the Conservative Party had needed a scapegoat and he had been selected on that occasion as scapegoat No. 1. He told his audience that on 5 July (polling day) he would be returned to the obscurity from which he had emerged, that he knew his place and he only wished Mr Churchill was able to understand it, adding that Churchill was really in a curiously interesting position. The constitution of the Labour Party, Laski said, had been published in 1918, and had been available to Churchill since that date. Either he had never read it, so that the stunt was the outcome of wanton ignorance, or alternatively it was a piece of deliberate misrepresentation.

'I suggest', Laski went on, 'the real truth is, the incredibly simple truth, the Tory Party has arrived at the state where it does not know what to say about its own policy. I agree with every word of Mr Attlee's letter to the Prime Minister. It defines a position the Prime Minister knew perfectly well existed. It is shameful to think that a man who, up to VE Day had so eminent a reputation, should have stained that reputation by descending to matters of this kind.'

Laski was ever ready to pay tribute to Churchill as war-time leader and at the Victory Rally at the Central Hall had told his audience: 'On the day his rule as Prime Minister draws to a close I want in the name of the British Labour Party to thank Mr Churchill for the great service he has rendered to this nation.'

When Attlee returned from Potsdam he found another letter awaiting him from Laski. It read:

> Let me first of all wish you the strength and power to carry through your immense task. I have often criticised you. However, I think you know that this has been the unpersonal judgement of political difference. Here I want to say what I said at the national executive on Tuesday, that whatever support by loyalty can bring to aiding the Government I will give gladly and proudly. No one knows better than I that if we all stand firm we may open a great epoch in the history of civilisation.
>
> I hope when you come to consider these things that you will find a way of using me at the Embassy in Washington. I do know America with a quite special intimacy. I have a good many friends all over the country, and I think I could do, not least with ordinary people, the kind of job interpreting Great Britain to the United States which Bryce did in his day. I venture to feel that, after twenty-five years in the service of the Party, it is not unreasonable, especially after this election, to hope that you will make it realised that the Party has not regarded my efforts on its behalf as insignificant. I know I could do a good job in Washington and I care for that more than anything else. But at least I want the Beaverbrooks and the Brackens to know that my own Party does not regard me as a leper it would not touch.

The only action Attlee took was to once more write to Laski, as on a previous occasion, to say that his letter had been noted. And Attlee asked Lord Halifax to remain British Ambassador in Washington.

Laski continued to be in demand as a platform speaker and with the Labour Party in power considerable publicity was given both at home and abroad to his speeches, especially on foreign affairs. He was referred to, of course, as 'Chairman of the British Labour Party' in the foreign Press and it is understandable that it was not always appreciated overseas that he was not a member of the Government. During the first few weeks of the new Government Laski, a keen student of the international scene, spread his topics across almost the whole range of foreign affairs. He questioned the Government's policy on India, said what its attitude should be towards France, what line should be adopted towards Spain and the Far East and suggested the policy the United States should adopt towards Great Britain. He talked about British policy towards Greece and said what should be done to help the people of China. When he was reported in Sweden as having referred to Great Britain as a second-class power he issued a Press statement on his return to London saying that it was 'no more than a perhaps poor attempt at humour'. The newspapers continued to be ever ready to report whatever Laski said, including casual asides which did not always convey in cold print the circumstances in which they were uttered.

The Labour Government had not been in office a month when Attlee felt obliged to write to Laski in the following terms:

My Dear Harold,
Your letter has just reached me and I hope you will make useful contacts in the Scandinavian countries. I thank you also for your kindly reference in your *Reynolds* article. I am, however, bound to point out to you that the constant flow of speeches from and interviews with you are embarrassing. As Chairman of the Labour Party Executive you hold an important office in the Party and the position is not well understood abroad. Your utterances are taken to express the views of the Government.

You have no right whatever to speak on behalf of the Government. Foreign affairs are in the capable hands of Ernest Bevin. His task is quite sufficiently difficult without the embarrassment of irresponsible statements of the kind you are making.

I had hoped to have seen you but you were away in Paris. I can assure you there is widespread resentment in the Party at your activities and a period of silence on your part would be welcome.
                                                  Yours ever, Clem

It was at this time that an academic colleague, H. L. Beales, Reader in Economic History at the London School of Economics, wrote an article in a popular journal about Laski in which he said, reviewing Laski's activities as a professor-politician 'in our world of violence and brutalities, of waste and tension, of obsolete privilege and customary tolerance and widely prevalent kindliness Laski simply cannot live in an ivory tower. He has to do things...'. Lance Beales went on to write about his colleague's wide-ranging personal service and to pay tribute to his motives and principles. When Laski saw the article he was moved to write to Beales: 'When you are out on as slender a limb on as high a tree as I am, the friend who tells you to have courage is a friend indeed. I would like to say what I felt about your piece but I don't know how to do so. I will only say that it is absurdly generous but it has been a great tonic to know that I have at least one colleague who believes in me....'

A few days after he received Attlee's letter Laski had a very cordial welcome when he addressed the annual conference of the Trades Union Congress at Blackpool. However, during the remaining months of his chairmanship of the Labour Party his name appeared less frequently in the columns of the world's Press but he did, from time to time, still make the headlines. One such occasion was when he said to a New York audience: 'We have come to the boundaries of the final dividing line between Liberalism and Socialism. There is no middle way. Free enterprise and market economy mean war; Socialism and planned economy mean peace. All attempts to find a compromise are a satanic illusion. We must plan our civilisation or we perish.' He asserted that 'our schools and colleges, our universities and foundations, even the churches, are the instruments of big business' and described the existing form of economy in the United States as 'the direct road to serfdom'. Laski was speaking at a dinner in a New York hotel which was picketed by Roman Catholics (including two priests) who were protesting against declarations he had made in a speech to Spanish refugees which, they claimed, had insulted their Church.

As an example of the misunderstanding there was abroad as to Laski's influence when he was Chairman of the Labour Party it is interesting to note that on his death in 1950 one New York daily newspaper in an obituary notice spoke of Laski's 'own Party which he had brought into control of the British Parliament during his chairmanship in 1945-46'.

Laski's swan-song as Labour Party chairman was his presiding over the 1946 annual conference when he was most generous with his tributes to the Prime Minister and the Foreign Secretary. He spoke warmly of Ernest Bevin 'for the unresting zeal he has brought to a very complicated task' and, referring to a conference speech by Attlee said 'never in the long years of his career have I heard leadership more determined or vision more wide than the determination and vision that characterised the speech of the Prime Minister, our comrade Clement Attlee'. He concluded his presidential address with the words:

We all know that the age of socialist planning has arrived; the only issue that remains uncertain is whether those who fear its advent are likely to be wise enough to co-operate in its peaceful application. I think the chance is high that they will take this view in Britain. I think this is so because our people has a long experience of political freedom, and a social maturity that, as the war showed, has stood them in good stead in dangerous times. I do not seek to underestimate the perils of the road before us; I do not even pretend that our own generation can enter the promised land. But I believe, with all my heart, that if all the men and women in this movement not only feel about it deeply, but also think about it greatly, we can, in the next years, build the foundations of an experiment in the good life to which posterity will look back with admiration. I covet for our Party, even more I covet for our country, the ability to pioneer in a full socialist achievement as we pioneered in the definition of Socialist principles. If we are still hardly out of the Valley of the Shadow of Death, we have begun to climb the Mountains of Hope. Let us remember that the more the energy with which we advance, the more hope and courage this stricken world will find in our example. Let us, therefore, with high hearts and unbreakable courage, march on to the Socialist Commonwealth.

When, during the concluding minutes of the conference, Laski was thanking the Press, he turned to the reporters' table and speaking of 'the devoted attention they have given to my activities' commented: 'Never in the history of mankind have so many followed just one. The skeleton now goes back to the cupboard. As I come to the end of this year I go from the position in which the Press has placed me back to the obscurity of the academic tower where I dwell.'

During his year as Chairman of the Labour Party Laski was inundated with invitations from the continent and, always anxious to meet European colleagues, he accepted as many as he felt able to fit in. One of these was from the Italian Socialist Party to visit their country and he made the journey in April 1946. Laski's travelling companions, in addition to his wife, were Harry Earnshaw, a north country textile union official and Denis Healey who had, only a few months previously, joined the headquarters staff of the Labour Party as International Secretary.

When the party arrived in Milan they noticed that the city was decorated with red and white flags (the colours of the city) and on inquiring the reason were told that the socialists had just won a victory at the municipal elections. Their visit was thus singularly appropriate, and Laski in particular, who was looked upon as a leading figure in British socialism, was given a rousing reception. In Turin the next day Laski was most cordially greeted and at the end of a speech at a meeting of Italian workers he invited questions. As he was speaking in English he answered through an interpreter. One questioner asked when the British were intending to release Italian prisoners of war and let them come back home. Laski replied, facetiously, that perhaps these young men were enjoying themselves so much in England (and he mentioned English girls) that they did not want to return home. However, feeling that the audience might not appreciate the light-hearted way in which Laski had dealt with the question the Italian interpreter diplomatically gave a non-commital answer.

The party then travelled to Florence and Laski was approached by a Jew who implored him to visit Spezia harbour where some hundreds of Jews on their way to Palestine were being kept prisoners by the authorities and prevented from starting their sea journey. The result was they were threatening to go on hunger strike. Laski readily agreed and a correspondent in Italy has told me how, with hundreds of Jewish men and women on the quayside, Laski boarded the ship and went down into a cabin lighted only by a single hurricane lamp. After several hours of bargaining he promised to ask the British Government to intercede if they would call off their threatened hunger strike. 'It was an eerie sight', I was told, 'with the Jews on the quay-side fervently singing hymns, their eyes glistening in the semi-darkness.' In Florence Laski immediately made representations to the British Consul who sent a telegram to Ernest Bevin, the Foreign Secretary, with the result that the Jewish immigrants were allowed to continue their journey.

When Denis Healey learned that I was writing this book he very kindly invited me to meet him in his room at the Treasury.

The Chancellor of the Exchequer spoke with warmth and affection of Frida and Harold Laski. He relived some of his experiences in Italy and I recall him commenting how well Laski got on with Harry Earnshaw, one a veteran down-to-earth north countryman, the other a product of Oxford and a distinguished academic. Incidentally, Herbert Morrison once rebuked a parliamentary colleague who was denouncing Laski as 'just an intellectual'. 'There is a difference', Morrison said, 'between intellectuals who rise *with* the Labour movement and those who rise *on* it. I object to those who rise on the movement but Laski rose with it.'

Healey told me that, in Rome, Harry Earnshaw and he had an audience with the Pope. At the end of the interview the Pope opened a drawer in his table and took out two rosaries which he blessed, one black and one white. Turning to Earnshaw he said that whilst he was not of the faith he might like to take one back to England, and asked: 'Which colour would you like?' Earnshaw who, of course, had many Catholics amongst his Lancashire union members stretched out his hand and said: 'I think I'll take 'em both, your Holiness.' And he did!

Earlier in the interview Earnshaw had been telling the Pope about his work as a Lancashire textile union official and as a member of the Labour Party executive and the Pope commented: 'You must have big responsibilities, Mr Earnshaw.' To which he replied: 'Yes, your Holiness, and so have you.'

Also in 1946 Laski was a member of a Labour Party delegation which visited the Soviet Union and his companions were Morgan Phillips (Labour Party General Secretary), Harold Clay (of the Transport and General Workers' Union) and Alice Bacon, MP. Of the four who made the journey only Miss Bacon (now Lady Bacon) is still alive and living in retirement in Yorkshire. Anxious to have some first-hand impressions of the visit I approached Lady Bacon and I was disappointed when she replied that she was being urged to write a book which would include references to the 1946 Russian visit. She said she would not want what she had to say to appear in another book first and was, therefore, unable to help me. I had, therefore, to be content with the matter-of-fact official report of the delegation which, whilst it covers the occasion, does not include the sort of personal experiences and impressions that are invariably part of overseas visits and bring a factual account to life. They visited the places which are usually shown to foreign delegations, including, of course, Leningrad, Stalingrad and Moscow, were everywhere given the customary VIP treatment and returned home with generous gifts from their hosts.

There can be no doubt that one of the highlights of the tour was a two-hour meeting with Marshal Stalin in his room at the Kremlin. It was an informal affair with the Soviet leader communicative and relaxed. The delegation's first impression was that he was smaller and somewhat older than they had expected but his 'merry smile and twinkling eyes welcomed us before he had uttered a word'. They sat round a table to talk with Laski between Stalin and Dekendzov, the Third Secretary, who was in charge because Molotov and Vishinsky were in Paris. He had met and greeted the British party when they initially arrived in the Soviet Union.

Stalin was interested to know what had happened in Britain since the Labour Government had come to power just a year earlier, expressing surprise that Churchill had lost the election and saying that he had not thought such a result possible. He said he was gratified that their two countries were travelling in the socialist direction and commented that Russia was travelling a shorter but more difficult way. The Russians did not think theirs was the only road to socialism.

The Russian leader said he felt that the Labour Government had adopted the right line in dealing with the public ownership of the basic industries first but he said he would like to know what were the dangers of reaction from the political enemies of the Labour movement and from the industrialists who were dispossessed as the result of the action by the Government. That, he felt, was a contingency against which the Labour Government would have to be on their guard and he referred to the return to power of people whom it had been contended would never again be in a position of power and authority in the State. From their experience in Russia, Stalin said, they knew that if basic industries and commerce rested in the hands of the State, the State could direct its policy to reduce prices and raise real wages. In those fields in which commerce was not directly under the State, policy could be influenced by State action and this would be to the workers' advantage.

In the development of industrialisation, Stalin said, particularly in the early stages, they in the Soviet Union had experienced great difficulty. They had a peasant population much greater and in many ways different from that in Britain. To win them over to an understanding of socialist objectives was a difficult task; much care and thought had been given to the many problems which arose. Problems of a different order arose so far as the industrial workers were concerned but these were overcome. For a time a considerable proportion of the women were not active industrially. As that situation changed it had had a great effect upon their economy and the role now occupied by women was vitally important in the building of socialism. Stalin said that so far as domestic reconstruction was concerned, there was, and would continue to be, the fullest understanding between their two countries and he felt that in international affairs they could get the same degree of understanding. Russia, he said, would welcome the opportunity of the fullest co-operation between their two peoples. The many gifts Laski brought back from the Soviet Union included a bronze statuette of Lenin, presented to him by Nikolai Shvernik, President of the USSR.

Morgan Phillips later referred in a newspaper article to difficulties which had confronted interpreters arising from Laski's style of speaking and this prompted a correspondent to relate incidents during the visit. He wrote:

> I was at that time working at the British Embassy there. I remember accompanying the then Ambassador, the late Sir Maurice Peterson, to a reception given by a Soviet organisation in honour of the visiting delegation. Though many of the Russians present understood English it was often left to me to explain to them the significance of Laski's aphorisms and epigrams.
>
> One Russian in particular was bombarding him with questions about various prominent persons. I recall such replies as 'So-and-so has been sitting on the fence so long that the iron has entered his soul'; 'Mr Baldwin had the Englishman's gift of appearing to be an amateur in a game in which he was, in fact, a superb professional' and, of an American prominent in English life 'So-and-so is really just America's revenge on George III'. I discovered subsequently that he had used all these utterances on previous occasions and in quite other contexts.
>
> Perhaps the evening's neatest piece of wit came from an Englishman who, seeing Laski surrounded by a group of Russians and talk-

ing volubly, remarked to me: 'There's Laski, casting his usual imitation pearls before real swine.'

It is worth recalling that when a Russian made a somewhat disparaging allusion to Mr Churchill, whose famous speech, delivered shortly before in America, roused such hostile comment in Russia Laski warmly joined in his defence. He insisted that Mr Churchill was a great leader, for whose services in the war the Russians had good cause to be grateful.

At the time of Laski's death four years later, Morgan Phillips, referring to this visit to the Soviet Union, said that it was here that Laski: 'Met with one of the great disappointments of his life. He had the highest hopes for he believed sincerely that much of the mistrust and conception entertained by the Soviet leaders concerning Great Britain could be quickly dispelled by a personal contact. With the other delegates he was well aware that the Labour Party had nothing in common with Russian methods but he believed nevertheless that the Soviet government were working for a continued rise in the standard of life of the Russian people and that if they could be genuinely convinced of the goodwill of democratic Britain they might, by sheer example, be persuaded to adopt a different attitude to the world in general and ourselves in particular. Despite the fact that events moved in precisely the opposite direction he never gave up hope of a new approach. But the conditions of that approach were the democratic ones of free and open discussion and debate and he followed those conditions faithfully.'

CHAPTER SEVEN

ACTION FOR LIBEL

When, during the 1945 General Election campaign, Laski began to address a public meeting at Newark in Nottinghamshire it must have seemed to him to be just another of the sixty gatherings at which he spoke during the weeks leading up to polling day. It was, however, destined to have serious and far-reaching consequences for him.

It was on the evening of Saturday 16 June that he spoke in the Newark market-place in support of the Labour candidate, Air Vice-Marshal H. V. Champion de Crespigny, and at the end of the meeting he was questioned by a well-known journalist.

On the Monday morning the following letter appeared in the *Nottingham Guardian* signed by a Conservative member of the Nottinghamshire County Council:

> Sir,—
> Attending a meeting in the Newark Market Place on Saturday night I was horrified to hear Prof. Harold J. Laski, Chairman of the Socialist Party, when enumerating reforms he wanted to see, declare: 'If we cannot have them by fair means we shall use violence to obtain them.'
> A member of the audience immediately challenged him and said: 'You are inviting revolution from the platform.'
> Prof. Laski replied: 'If we cannot get reforms we desire we shall not hesitate to use violence, even if it means revolution.'
> I think the widest publicity should be given to this statement for I feel that electors all over the country should know what is really behind the Socialist mind.
> Seated on the platform was the Socialist candidate, Air Vice-Marshal Champion de Crespigny. I should like to know if this

Action for Libel

gallant gentleman does really associate himself with this statement, which he also heard.

> Yours faithfully,
> H. C. C. Carlton

Laski acted without delay and, late on the evening of Tuesday 19 June, the Press Association put out the following statement:

Mr Harold Laski referring tonight to a letter written to the *Nottingham Guardian* concerning Mr Laski's speech at Newark market-place last Saturday said: 'I am going to take out a writ for libel against the man who wrote it and against anybody else who reproduces the letter. My answer at the meeting was entirely different. What I said was: it was very much better to make changes in time of war when men were ready for great changes than to wait for the urgency to disappear through victory, and then to find that there was no consent to change what the workers felt an intolerable burden. That was the way that a society drifted to violence. We had it in our power to do by consent that which in other nations has been done by violence.'

Not surprisingly, the *Nottingham Guardian* letter came to the attention of Fleet Street, the *Daily Express* using a headline: 'Laski unleashes another general election broadside: socialism even if it means violence.'

On the Wednesday following the *Newark Advertiser* carried a report of Laski's main market-place speech (the accuracy of which was not subsequently challenged) and then came the following:

REVOLUTION BY VIOLENCE
Professor Laski Questioned:
There were some lively exchanges between Mr Wentworth Day and Professor Laski following the latter's speech in Newark Market Place on Saturday night. Mr Day asked the Professor why he had openly advocated 'revolution by violence' in speaking at Bishop's Stortford and Bournemouth during the war 'whilst most Englishmen were either fighting or being bombed at home' and why he had spent the whole of the last war lecturing in America. If he were unfit why did he not join the Red Cross?

REJECTED
Professor Laski replied that he was twice rejected in this country during the 1914–18 war and had medical certificates to prove it. He also attempted to enlist in Canada.... He also said, concerning the other part of the question, 'That was said about me in the House

of Commons ... and if you look at Hansard for the 29th November, 1944, you will see an ample and generous apology made to me for being as insolent as you are in suggesting it now.'

REFERENCE TO VIOLENCE
'As for violence,' he continued, if Labour could not obtain what it needed by general consent, 'we shall have to use violence even if it means revolution.' When people felt it was the moment for great experiment, for innovation, because when war is over people so easily forgot—especially those who had the power in their hands—that was the time for experiment. Great changes are so urgent in this country, that if they were not made by consent they would have to be made by violence, and judging by the temper his questioner had displayed he would perfectly naturally be one of the objects of the violence when it came.

Mr Day submitted to the Professor that when general consent was against him he substituted revolution.

Professor Laski said it did not lie in the mouth of any member of the Tory Party, who helped to organise mutiny in the British Army over Home Rule in 1914, to discuss the question of violence. When a situation in any society became intolerable—and when 25 per cent of the people had inadequate nutrition, it did become intolerable—it did not become possible to prevent what was not given by generosity being taken by the organised will of the people.

NOT AN ASSET
Mr Day: 'You are precisely the sort of bloodthirsty little man, full of words, who has never smelled a bullet, but is always the first to stir up violence in peace. We expect serious constructive thought from the Chairman of the Labour Party, but since you have consistently attacked everyone and everything from Mr Churchill to the leaders of your own Party and the Constitution of this country, and have been disowned by Mr Attlee only this morning, how can anyone take you seriously? I suggest that you are not an asset to the Labour Party but a liability.'

On 20 June Laski issued writs claiming damages for libel against the *Nottingham Guardian* and H. C. C. Carlton, and against the *Daily Express* and on the 22 June against the *Evening Standard* all based on the publication and reproduction of Mr Carlton's letter. On the 22 June he issued a writ against the *Newark Advertiser* and C. E. Parlby, as editor, based on its report of the questions and answers set out above and subsequently the

Action for Libel

action against the *Newark Advertiser* was set down for hearing first. As the outcome of that case was bound to have an effect on the others the *Daily Express* agreed to be responsible for the conduct of the action in the interests of all the defendants.

Laski's Statement of Claim was delivered on 6 July. It set out the words of the above report, except the last two paragraphs, and declared:

(a) that they were false and malicious;
(b) that, by innuendo, they meant and were understood to mean that Laski had declared his intention to commit and to conspire with others to commit the crimes of treason, treason felony, sedition, riot and breach of the peace if the policy of the Labour Party should not be put into operation by constitutional means and that Laski was guilty of treason felony; and
(c) that in consequence Laski had been injured in his character, credit and reputation and had been brought into public hatred, scandal and contempt;

At first the defence, delivered on 31 July was a formal one:

(a) that the words did not mean what was pleaded in the innuendo;
(b) that the report was a fair and accurate report of the proceedings of a public meeting within section 4 of the Law of Libel Amendment Act, 1888;
(c) that such parts of the report as were statements of fact were true, or were a fair and accurate report of proceedings at a public meeting, and such parts as were statements of opinion were fair comment— the rolled up plea with a variation.

The defence was amended on 16 April 1946 and it was pleaded that the words of the report were true in substance and in fact.

As the Labour Party won the General Election decisively there were those who held that Laski should not proceed with his action. However, he was advised that he had a good case and he was aware, too, that it had been said during the campaign that once the election was over he would not press the writs. Indeed the Lord Chancellor, Lord Simon, said at an election meeting at Carshalton that: 'If you wanted to stop people's mouths the way was to issue a writ. The most extraordinary thing about Professor Laski was that when he didn't like what someone said about him he issued a writ and treated the reason of issuing a writ as to why he should not explain anything. I'll bet you as soon as this election is over you won't hear anything more about these writs.'

A few days later Lord Simon wrote the following letter to Laski and sent a copy to the Press:

My attention has been called to a report of some words I used, when speaking at Carshalton in support of the candidature of Brigadier Head, in reference to writs you had issued during the election. The meeting was at times rather noisy, and what I said was unpremeditated and without notes; but I am not seeking to challenge the report at all.

While, of course, a Lord Chancellor would have nothing to do with hearing your cases, and, if there was an appeal, I should not sit, I feel that, having regard to the judicial side of my office, I ought not to have made these observations, and I am sorry that I did.

I have had no communication nor complaint from you, but I deem it my duty to write to express my regret, and I am sending this letter to the Press.

For a time after he had issued the writs Laski felt that he alone must meet the costs of the forthcoming High Court action (he could never have dreamed how things would turn out) and when he received a cheque from a 'well-wisher' who wanted to contribute to his legal expenses, Laski sent it to the Labour Party's election fund.

After very protracted preliminaries, the case opened in the Law Courts in London on 26 November 1946 before the Lord Chief Justice, Lord Goddard, and lasted five days. The defence asked for the case to be tried before a 'special jury', a jury of seven chosen from a special list in which were entered the names of persons possessing a property qualification higher than that required in the case of common jurors. The request was granted and there was a feeling in some quarters that this move on the part of the defence would mean that the case was to be tried by men of substance and financial standing who would be unlikely to by sympathetic to a man of Laski's socialist principles.

G. O. Slade, KC, Sir Valentine Holmes, KC, and Peter Bristow appeared for Laski whilst for the defendants Sir Patrick Hastings, KC, led Holroyd Pearce (later Justice Pearce), Arthian Davies (later Justice Davies) and A. L. Gordon.

In his opening statement G. O. Slade commented that it was one of the most serious actions for libel which had been before the courts 'for many a long day'. Referring to the words that had led to the action for libel 'As for violence, if Labour could not obtain what it needed by general consent we shall have to use violence, even if it means revolution' Slade said: 'Mr Laski never used those words or any words to that effect and I shall have to deal with that in due course. In fact, I believe I shall be able to show you how those three lines got into the report.' Later he said: 'I shall call before you some ten witnesses who were present at that meeting who will all deny that he used those words or any words to like effect' and it was disclosed as the case went on that the words were not in the notebook of the shorthand writer working for the *Newark Advertiser* who attended for the purpose of reporting the meeting but were later added to the report in the *Newark Advertiser* office from a note supplied by the man who questioned Laski, Day. Indeed, Sir Patrick Hastings himself, in his opening speech for the defence explained in some detail what had happened when he said:

> I will tell you how this ever came to be published at all. The *Newark Advertiser* in this district has a gentleman who can write shorthand, Mr Opie. Now you were told that we sent our special correspondent or our special reporter to go there and take down every word of this monumental speech. Mr Opie is the gentleman who goes in Newark to the local flower show, the local funeral, the local wedding, anything. He is the only one we have got and he goes round with his notebook and takes notes. There was nothing more interesting in Newark, you might think, than the political meeting at the time of the General Election, and that is why he was there with his notebook and he took a note which is absolutely accurate and admitted to be accurate with the exception of this one sentence, with which I am going to deal in a moment. This is how that came to be in. The person who asked the question was a Mr Wentworth Day. He had got nothing whatever to do with us; he was the editor at one time of *The Field* newspaper, a journalist, and he was engaged at this time as a sort of agent for the Conservative candidate; I do not even remember his name, but the gentleman opposing Air Vice-Marshal de Crespigny. I dare say you know perfectly well at political meetings it is the usual thing for the opponent's agent to go and heckle the speaker and in that capacity Mr Wentworth Day went along and heckled him. Mr Wentworth Day took down his answers; whether he took them down at the time or mentally I do not know, but you will hear a body of evidence of people who will tell you that every word that Mr Wentworth Day put in his report was right.
>
> Now how that sentence came to be in was thus. The editor of the

Newark Advertiser, whom you will hear, said to Mr Opie, 'Write out your shorthand note and let me see it.' At the same time Mr Wentworth Day sent in to the *Newark Advertiser* his version of what had taken place. I think this is the only local newspaper and naturally both sides, I suppose, wanted the good offices of the newspaper to the extent that they could get them. At any rate, Mr Wentworth Day either came in or sent in a note. When Mr Opie was writing out his note he saw, having read Mr Wentworth Day's note, this sentence, which is the disputed sentence, that Mr Day had put in and it was not in the words that Mr Opie had got down. Mr Parlby (the editor) thought it summarised it very accurately, cut it out and put it on the top. That is how those words came to be in: they came from Mr Wentworth Day, what is suggested to be a conspiracy about this I really do not know, but that is how they came to be in. I shall have to call before you Mr Wentworth Day, the editor, Mr Opie and all the people who can tell you exactly every word and how this came to be in.

Some idea of the ordeal which Laski underwent in the witness-stand may be judged by the fact that he was asked 74 questions by his own counsel during his examination-in-chief, a further 52 questions when re-examined, and over 370 questions by the opposing counsel Sir Patrick Hastings. It will be seen from this that it is not possible in this book to do more than select odd passages from his evidence which indicate the trend of the questioning.

Early in his examination-in-chief Slade asked Laski: 'Until Mr Wentworth Day started to ask you questions, whatever they were, in the Newark Market Place, or until you saw the *Nottingham Guardian* and the *Newark Advertiser*, had the suggestion ever been made to you that you were a person who advocated revolution by violence?'—'Never, to my knowledge, anywhere at any time.'

'If you were a person who advocated revolution by violence, could you be a member of the Labour Party?'—'No. By the constitution of the Labour Party, any member of the Labour Party is committed to the acceptance of constitutional democracy.'

'What has been your attitude towards Communism?'—'I have been a critic of Communism ever since 1920, when I returned to the University of London. In 1927 I published a book on Communism which contains strong criticism of communist theory and communist strategy, and recently, just before the late Bournemouth Conference of the Labour Party, I published, on behalf of the Labour Party a long attack in a pamphlet called *The Secret Battalion* against both communist theory and practice and the desire of the Communist Party to be admitted into membership of the Labour Party.'

'In what sense or senses have you used, and do you use, the word "revolution"?'—'In two senses; first, to describe as a normal figure of speech, large-scale changes in the social constitution of the country, and then in its technical sense of the violent dispossession of a ruling order under a given constitution from the possession of the authority they derive from the constitutional position.'

'What is your view and what view have you consistently expressed as to what I may call revolution in this country?'—'I have said, ever since I began to write, that if changes were effected in this country by violence, it would be disastrous, because it would result in the suppression of democratic government and with it all the good things, religious toleration, freedom of speech, the security of the person, and so forth, that are naturally and logically associated with constitutional government.'

'With regard to revolution by consent, which is the title of one of the essays or writings which are included in the Particulars of Justification here, what is your view about that?'—'My view and the meaning of that title is that where you can get the electorate of a national society like Great Britain to agree by the choice that they make upon the desirability of great changes and thereby, by true constitutional means, transform the social order towards what I regard as greater social justice, the benefit of change effected by consent of that character is overwhelmingly greater than any benefit that could be secured by coercion.'

When he began his cross-examination of Laski, Sir Patrick Hastings asked: 'Do you believe that the use of violence to achieve your political ends is practically inevitable?'—'No. In a country where there is a long constitutional tradition of mature and literate people, I think that consent—'

'Is the answer "No"?'—'The answer is "No".'

'As far as possible would you keep your answers short. Have you ever believed that which I have put to you?'—'No.'

'Do you agree with me that anyone who for years had preached such a doctrine would be a public danger?'—'No, not necessarily.'

'Have you preached it for years and years?'—'No.'
'Have you ever preached it?'—'No.'
'Have you ever preached it?'—'NO.'

'You do not think that such a person would be necessarily a public danger?'—'I do not understand quite what you mean by that.'

'Could you answer "Yes" or "No". Supposing a person for years were preaching his doctrine to a dissatisfied proletariat "The use of violence to achieve your political aims is practically inevitable" don't you think such a person would be a public danger?'—'That would depend upon the degree of his power to persuade those to whom he spoke.'

'You mean to say he might be useless and therefore not a danger, or powerful and then a danger?'—'Yes.'

'Would you consider yourself, with the innumerable qualifications which Sir Valentine Holmes read out to us, a person sufficiently powerful to be a public danger?'—'I should have said not.'

'In this court you would say not. On public platforms you take rather a different view, don't you?'—'I have never said on any public platforms anything that could be construed into a belief that I am a significant public figure in the national life.'

'Do you believe that, if the achievement of political aims cannot be arrived at without the use of violence, then violence is justifiable?'—'Not in all circumstances. In circumstances where the burden is intolerable, violence may be inevitable, because the burden is intolerable, but not otherwise.'

'In the circumstances which existed on 16 June 1945 the date you made this speech, did you then believe that, if the aims of the proletariat could not be achieved without the use of violence, then violence was justifiable?'—'No.'

'Do you agree that anyone who preached that doctrine would be a public danger?'—'Yes.'

'And have you preached it for 20 years?'—'No.'

'We shall see. If you have preached it for 20 years you agree you would be a public danger?'—'If I had preached to the proletariat the inevitability of violence for 20 years, I should certainly be a public danger.'

'And you would not complain of what was said about you in this action?'—'I should have complained of the untruth of the

Action for Libel

words attributed to me on the occasion, but not the general description that you were seeking to give to my personality.'

'We shall have to see whether you have been preaching.'—'If you please.'

Hastings then picked up a copy of Laski's book *A Grammar of Politics* and said: 'Just listen to this, will you? "The view I am concerned to urge is that from the standpoint of the state, the citizen must be left unfettered to express, either individually or in concert with others, any opinions he happens to hold. He may preach the complete inadequacy of the social order. He may demand its overthrow by armed revolution. He may insist that the political system is the apotheosis of perfection. He may argue that all opinions which differ from his own ought to be subject to the severest suppression." Do you agree with that?'—'Certainly.'

'Do you agree that for years before the date of this speech you had been writing continuously upon this—that the state of this country under what you described as capitalism is so bad that capitalism must go?'—'Yes. That is why I am a socialist.'

'And do you agree with this, that the social conditions are such that there must be a revolution either by consent or by violence?'—'Yes.'

After questioning Laski about another of his books Hastings asked: 'Have you consistently preached this doctrine, that the time is ripe for revolution?'—'The time is ripe for great changes.'

'Have you for years preached the doctrine that the time is ripe for revolution?'—'Revolution in the sense of great transformation always.'

'You have written many books in which the word revolution is contained, and you define it in your books. Have you preached the doctrine that this revolution may be brought about in one of two ways, either by consent, you call it a revolution by consent, or by revolution by violence?'—'That is so.'

'And by a revolution by consent do you mean this—because the enemy are always capitalists, are they not?'—'Broadly.'

'Do you mean that the enemy, if there is to be a consent, must in the very nature of things consent to their own elimination—that is to say, they have to consent to go?'—'They have to consent to great changes.'

'I have in front of me, and I have read, some twenty, thirty or forty different publications of yours, so I know something about them. Have you stated that what you mean by a revolution by consent is that the capitalists must consent to their total erosion? That is your word. I thought it might have meant "elimination" but you say "erosion".'—'No. I do not mean by what I have said the elimination of capitalists.'

'What do you mean by the word "erosion"?'—'Erosion means rubbing away.'

'How do you consent to rub yourself away?'—'By fading out of the picture in which you have been previously the most prominent part.'

'By disappearing?'—'Yes.'

'Consent to their own disappearance?'—'To their loss of power.'

During the cross-examination, Hastings had on a number of occasions pressed Laski to answer 'Yes' or 'No' rather than give lengthy explanations and on one occasion Laski turned to Lord Goddard for guidance as to whether he should answer such a question by 'Yes' or 'No'. If he did, Laski said, it would give a totally false impression. Lord Goddard told Laski he was entitled to give an explanation of his answers but he (Lord Goddard) did not want the case turned into a history of the socialist creed.

When Hastings asked Laski 'Are there any privileged in the Socialist Party' the reply was: 'Why indeed, Sir Patrick, when you were a member....' He was, however, not permitted to finish the sentence, the judge declaring: 'No, Mr Laski.' This, of course, reminded the court that Laski was being ruthlessly cross-examined by a former Attorney General in a Labour Government.

Towards the end of the second day Hastings turned to the actual meeting at Newark and it was here that he got answers that led him to conclude the cross-examination. He said he wanted to see how far the words to which Laski objected varied from what he agreed was substantially accurate reporting. Turning to the newspaper he read: 'Great changes are so urgent in this country, and if they were not made by "consent"—now those were the changes to be made by consent and you have described in your books so often what you mean by consent—"they would be made by violence". You said that?'—'I think so.'

'"They would be made by violence"—by whose violence?'—'By the drift of events in the country.'

'Who was going to drift?'—'The whole country would drift

Action for Libel

into a situation where agreement between parties would be suspended.'

'Very well. Let us assume all that. Who would use violence to bring about these changes?'—'My view is the view I have consistently affirmed, that a Labour Government would obtain the power, would be challenged and would have to suspend the Constitution, that the outcome of its suspension would nevertheless be its successful government, and by the successful government it would operate the changes for which it was elected.'

'I do wish you would try, if you could, Mr Laski, to answer my questions a little more shortly.'—'I am doing my best, Sir Patrick, but you are trying to confine me in a narrower compass than is justified by the fact.'

At this point Lord Goddard intervened, saying: 'Just read the whole passage, Mr Laski, beginning "When people felt it was the moment of great experiment..." You are being asked, in view of that, when you say that if they are not made by consent, they will be made by violence, you mean it would be made by violence by the people who make the experiment?'—'Certainly.'

Resuming his cross-examination, Hastings said: 'That is all I am asking you. Now let us just see just what that means, Mr Laski. This is what you are saying, what you admit you are saying: If these socialistic changes are not made by consent they will be made by the violence of those who believe in socialism?'—'Yes.'

'But where in the world does that differ from what you say in the passage of which you complain? I cannot follow it. Is it not exactly the same?'—'No.'

'Is there some dialectic difference between the two? Let me read it to you again. I will read the two passages side by side. This is what you admit you said: "Great changes were so urgent in this country, and if they were not made by consent they would be made by violence"—by the violence of those who believed in socialism. That is what you said. Now this is what you complain of: "If Labour could not obtain what it needed by general consent Labour will make them by the use of violence." Why is that not exactly the same thing? I cannot follow it.'—'It is not exactly the same thing because the whole of the speech was a plea for making changes by consent. I am made to mean in the passage I complain of that we shall move to making them by violence.'

'Someone heckled you and he asked you what you meant by

saying that you believed in violence—something to that effect—and this is how you answered. You said: "Great changes were so urgent in this country, and if they were not made by consent they would be made by the violence of the socialist supporters." That is what you said, is it not?'—'Yes.'

'Then where in the world does that differ from the passage of which you complain in which it is said: "If Labour could not obtain what it needed by general consent"—that is socialists getting what they want by consent—"we", that is they, the socialist party, would have to use violence. Why is it not exactly the same? I do not follow the distinction.'—'The distinction is the distinction between the operation of normal constitutional processes and the suspension of those processes.'

When Hastings continued to press Laski on the point, Lord Goddard intervened to say: 'May I suggest you have got the words, Sir Patrick, and you have made your point. Now cannot we pass on.' After Hastings had addressed a few more questions to Laski, Lord Goddard intervened again to say: 'I shall, of course, have to tell the jury that the meaning of the words is for them. The jury will have to make up their minds what the words mean.' With this Hastings indicated that he had no more questions to ask.

Ten witnesses were called to give evidence in support of Laski's claim that he did not use the words: 'If Labour cannot obtain what it needs by general consent we shall have to use violence even if it means revolution.' They were led by Air Vice-Marshal H. V. Champion de Crespigny, the Labour Party candidate on whose behalf Laski was speaking. He said: 'I am quite sure that Professor Laski did not make that statement, otherwise I should have paid particular attention to it.' Those who followed to the witness-stand included E. K. Walker, the Labour Party's election agent, E. G. Walker, chairman of the market-place meeting, and O. Essame who said that if he had heard Laski use the words complained of 'in my capacity as member of the Notts. County Bench and Newark Bench I should have thought it my duty to lodge a very strong protest in honour of my oath to the King'.

Sir Patrick Hastings called seven witnesses for the defence. They were C. E. Parlby, editor of the *Newark Advertiser*; J. Opie, the newspaper reporter who attended the meeting; J. W. Day, who questioned Laski; R. A. S. Breene, Acting British Consul in

Trebizond; H. C. C. Carlton who wrote the letter to the *Nottingham Guardian*; Viscount Hinchingbrooke, who gave evidence as to taking part in a broadcast talk with Laski; and B. J. Spinks. Then followed the final speeches of Sir Patrick Hastings and Slade and the judge's summing up.

Towards the end of his summing up, and after he had reviewed the evidence of the witnesses, Lord Goddard said:

Professor Laski, on the one hand says: 'My view has been and my feeling has been pessimistic, if you like; I may be a pessimist; I may think that the thing is inevitable; but I have not advocated the use of violence; I have not advocated the use of rebellion. I have, on the other hand, pointed out what would follow.'

On the other hand the Defendants say: 'By your language you have incited and advocated rebellion and violence and the like.' A man may always express his opinions provided that he avoids defamation, blasphemy, obscenity and does not fall, on the other side, into what I may call the pit of sedition.

Members of the Jury, the line is a fine one; it is often difficult to draw. It is because it is so difficult to draw that it is eminently a question for a jury to pass upon; for, as I said to you at the opening of my summing up when I started to charge you, the law of England is that a man may say that which the jury think is expedient. He may not say what a jury may think is inexpedient to say, provided they have been properly charged as to when a thing may become expedient or when it may be inexpedient. You may say as a matter of your political creed that you hate this and you hate that; you may say that I believe in a political theory, and my political theory is that if you do not take this or that course, certain results may follow; but you must not use language which can be fairly taken as an incitement to violence and to lead to revolution.

Saying that it was eminently a matter of common sense, he went on:

You must, however, use your own judgement and your own common sense and must think whether these various matters which have been put before you, these speeches and so forth, remembering the audience to which they are addressed, would be an incitement to violence or revolution, whether it is preaching revolution and violence as part of a political creed and urging people to adopt it. If you think it is, then, of course, what was said by the Defendants would probably be true. But on the other hand, you have to remember, as I have said before, that Professor Laski is entitled to state what his political creed is, if he is stating it not as a matter of incitement and not as a matter of advocacy but as a matter of argument, and putting forward views which you or other people may abominate and hate, but which he is at liberty to express and has the right to express, then he has constitutional rights of free discussion. I can put the matter no higher to you. I hope I have not left out anything.

After the judge's summing up the jury were out for only forty minutes before returning with their verdict. They found that the report in the *Newark Advertiser* was a fair and accurate report of a public meeting, dealing with a matter of public concern and published for the public benefit. This rendered unnecessary any further consideration of the issue of justification and judgement was entered for the *Newark Advertiser* with costs. Later Laski made it known that he did not intend to proceed with the actions against the other newspapers.

Faced with a bill of costs amounting to £13,000, Laski spoke of the possibility of having to sell his house and library. However, the Labour Party issued an appeal and the money was soon raised, most of it coming in small sums from rank and file members of the Labour Party and from the United States. Expressing his gratitude, Laski said: 'I wish to give thanks to socialists in Britain, France, many countries in Europe and in the USA for their generosity to me in what has been a hard and difficult experience.' Making his first appearance after the hearing of the libel action he was welcomed with prolonged applause when he presided at a Fabian Society jubilee lecture in the Central Hall, Westminster. With the speaker, J. B. Priestley, by his side and obviously moved by the reception, Laski said: 'I go on serving the movement so long as it wants me and so long as I have the strength.'

Laski himself described the result of the libel action as 'a bitter blow'. He felt he had been publicly humiliated. I understand that he had been advised at the time that he had a very good case and excellent prospects of succeeding in his action.

When Lord Goddard died in 1971 (at the age of ninety-four) references were made in the Press to the libel action and his attitude to the case particularly when Laski was on the witness-stand. There were those who felt at the time—and these views were reiterated in 1971—that Goddard showed where his sympathies lay when—for instance—he pulled Laski up sharply when, on the witness-stand, he reminded Hastings that he had at one time been a Law Officer in the 1924 Labour Government. In politics Goddard was a strong Conservative and in 1929 he unsuccessfully sought election to the House of Commons.

When passing on to Morgan Phillips, General Secretary of the Labour Party, a cheque for £100 received from an old student towards the costs of the libel action, Laski wrote: 'I have been comforted a little by the mass of letters I have received from quite unknown lawyers apologising to me for the profound partisanship of the judge and the usual helplessness of any socialist who falls into the hands of a special jury in London.'

Laski's brother, Neville, himself a QC and Judge of the Liverpool Crown Court, has placed it on record that in 1965 Lord Goddard approached him in the Smoking Room of the Benchers' Suite in the Inner Temple and asked him: 'Was your brother very grieved and angry with me for my conduct of his libel action?' When Neville Laski replied that he knew his brother was badly hurt Goddard continued: 'The reason I am speaking of this is very important to me personally. I have never worried about a case as I have tried so much as this. Lately there has been a revival of this case on the wireless and I have received numerous letters, mostly critical, some of which I have answered. I did not agree with the finding of the jury.' Neville Laski said that Goddard then went on to make some highly critical observations on some of the evidence for the defence and continued: 'I gravely considered whether there was anything I could do but as a jury was involved I was helpless. I have been unhappy about this case always and often think about it. I can say that it has been on my conscience. I do want to add that your brother was not a good witness. He could not answer simply "yes" or "no" and made long speeches. Slade was no match for Pat Hastings.' This conversation was set down in writing by Neville Laski at the time at the suggestion of H. P. Levy, a fellow-barrister, who included it in a letter published in *The Times* on 12 June 1971 in which he said that 'doubtless Professor Laski would have felt some satisfaction and even a sense of vindication by such frankness'.

CHAPTER EIGHT

FAMILY MAN

It was of incalculable help to Laski that, throughout his academic and political life, he had his wife, Frida, by his side. I only got to know her when she was ninety years old and whilst I was writing this book. She talked to me, with an obvious deep affection, of their forty years together, of the friends they had made and their journeyings at home and abroad. It is now twenty-five years since her husband died but she speaks of him with a warmth and affection that a quarter of a century has done nothing to lessen. Many people who have talked to me remember Frida and Harold Laski in other days and they have spoken of what they obviously meant to each other and, knowing how critical some people were of him, how she was ever ready to spring to his defence. An American lady who had opportunities of seeing the Laskis in their home said to me, 'it was Mrs Laski's part to care for her husband's health and the comfort of his frail body as well as she was allowed, and it was clear she devoted herself entirely to him'. Another American commented 'she really used to worship him', and a correspondent who spent a long week-end at the Laskis' home wrote to me of 'a deep loving relationship between Frida and Harold Laski' and of 'a tenderness of look, word and consideration for each other unsurpassed in my lifetime'. In a letter to his American friend Holmes, in 1923, Laski said: 'A perfect day on which to write to you for today I have been married twelve years and I feel as though I were still in the faint early flush of an idyll. You can guess what such years of perfect comradeship have meant. Certainly I have been blessed as few others in these matters.' As we have seen he suffered bouts of ill-health throughout his life and when from time to time he had to admit that he could go on no longer it fell to his wife to nurse him back to health and to try to prevent him from returning to work too soon. Referring once to 'the glory of love and friendship' Laski said 'of the first I do not speak; its beauty defies the written word'. When he wrote *The American Democracy* he dedicated the book to his wife, saying in the preface that his doing so meant 'far more than its words imply. But there is gratitude too intimate even to search for expression'.

Of course, one of the great joys of the Laskis' life was their daughter Diana, born in 1916, whilst they were in Montreal. Diana (her middle name was Maitland after the legal historian whom her father greatly admired) met her husband at a street coffee-stall when they were both at Oxford in 1935, she was reading history at Lady Margaret Hall, having previously been at St Paul's Girls' School in London and the London School of Economics. Her husband Robin Matthewson, told me:

We soon became firm friends and her father helped me financially so that I could study during vacations. I used to visit the family at their cottage at Little Bardfield in Essex and I recall that her parents, with Diana and I, used to make a foursome at tennis which Mr Laski played very well, left-handed. He was also a maniac for the game of Monopoly but most of the time he sat in his armchair writing that year's book and smoking cigarettes. Diana and I both graduated in 1938. Mr Laski put me on to a vacancy in the classics department at Harvard so I went to the United States and Diana studied at near-by Radcliffe College. The following spring we were married. Just before the outbreak of war in 1939 we returned to London where I became senior classics master at St Paul's School with a break for national service. In the early 1950s we moved to Exeter where we spent fifteen very happy years (with our four sons) until my wife's death in 1969. During her last years she was confirmed into the Church of England thus finding something that gave her great happiness and contentment. She became secretary of a local Christian society and spent a lot of time doing voluntary work helping elderly people.

An American clergyman, the Rev. Donald Lothrop, told me that he officiated at the marriage of Laski's daughter, Diana to Robin Matthewson, on 29 May 1939. Her parents were not present at the ceremony which was conducted outdoors at the home of Dr Day in Cambridge, Massachusetts, he being a friend of the family. Mr Lothrop said that, instead of accepting an honorarium for his services, he asked Diana if she would persuade her father to occupy the pulpit of the Community Church in Boston sometime when he was in the United States. He explained to me that from the outset of the founding of the Church over fifty years ago it had a different conception of the pulpit from that of the conventional established church and that 'a new idea of co-operative specialists was sought so that its pulpit could represent a wide range of interests. No one denomination was to be in control and no one man's point of view, however stimulating, was to be exclusively represented. The ideal was to have a community pulpit to which men of all types and experiences could be invited'. I have seen a most impressive list of hundreds of men and women who have accepted invitations over the years and they include statesmen and political leaders, theologians and philosophers, trade union leaders, economists, sociologists, political scientists, editors, lawyers and jurists. Diana promised to approach her father but the war intervened and when Mr Lothrop heard that Laski was in America in 1948 he wrote to him renewing the invitation and reminding him of the circumstances in which he had first made the approach. Laski, however, replied: 'Although I appreciate these kind invitations that you send me from time to time I think I ought to say frankly and definitively that I make it a rule that never under any circumstances do I speak under any auspices that are religious in character. Accordingly I fear that even if I were to return to the United States there is no prospect of my being able to visit you.'

No one who knew Laski would have been surprised at his reply to Mr Lothrop's invitation. We have already seen his reaction to the introduction of the most modest religious practices at the London School of Economics. Although he spent his early days in an orthodox Jewish home, religious ritual and dogma never meant anything to him from his boyhood. In later life he said that he had never seen a church movement that had sufficient faith in its principles to fight for justice. They were not, he consistently argued, interested in a practical way in questions of social justice. He claimed that their emphasis on the promise of a life hereafter (for which, Laski stressed, he had never seen any evidence) had done much to divert men and women from what was needed to be done on earth in the way of social reform and the prevention of the continued exploitation of the mass of people.

The attitude of the Church had invariably been to the advantage of those people who enjoyed privilege. Addressing a Labour women's rally in Durham, Laski once said that Socialism was the very soul of religion itself. He told his audience that if there was anyone who said he was a Christian but owed no allegiance to the Socialist party then he might profess Christianity with his lips but he denied it with his heart.

Throughout his career Laski was known to his friends to be 'something of a romancer' and although he was certainly on close personal terms with many distinguished men and women there was some doubt as to whether all the conversations he spoke about actually took place just as he said. This embroidering of stories was always something of a puzzle to his friends but, in fact, they learned to expect and accept it. As one of his colleagues put it 'his desire to dramatise a good story led him to an over-artistic arrangement of its incidentals'. It was a foible that seems to have remained with him throughout his life but it must be emphasised that he never invented anything in the least degree malicious or hurtful to anybody. Whilst newcomers to his wide circle of acquaintances understandably accepted everything he had to say with complete confidence, more familiar friends learned by experience just how much weight to attach to the details of some of his anecdotes.

'I don't think Laski knew when he was romancing if it concerned himself in relation to great men or great events', Eric Sevareid, of the Columbia Broadcasting System of America, told me. He went on:

Ed. Murrow, the radio commentator, and I called to see him at his London home shortly after the end of the last war and he gave us to understand that he had accompanied Winston Churchill on his triumphal visit to Paris after its liberation. Not only that, he gave us the firm impression that he was with Churchill when he called on Madame Foch. 'She came', Laski told us, 'down the stairway almost overcome with tears. Unable to speak she handed Churchill a note which said: "Were the Marshal alive he would not have done as Petain did."' Laski would have us believe he was at Churchill's side all through this and, of course, it cannot be true.

John Hutchinson, now of Washington, DC, in recalling his London days as a student of Laski, told me:

I remember his reporting a lunch with Mr Molotov when, in fact,

Mr Molotov had left for Moscow the day before the lunch evidently took place, but perhaps it was we who misunderstood. One of the 'games' at the London School of Economics was to compare the castes and denouements of the stories he told year by year. They varied but the stories were so good it hardly seemed to matter. I have no doubt that the search for point was often more diligent than that for precision, and that, like all great raconteurs, Laski always had to beat himself. But we lost nothing of the truth and in any case came to love his passion for ideas and his compassion.

Quincy Wright, a fellow-tutor of Laski's at Harvard who kept in touch with him over the years that followed has recalled:

A colleague of mine told me that once, whilst visiting Laski in London, no distinguished personage, whether in the fields of politics, science or literature could be mentioned but what Laski would say 'Yes, I was talking with him yesterday' or 'I had a letter from him a week ago'. It was the last straw when my friend remarked that he had just bought a Burberry and Laski said: 'Oh yes, Burberry is my uncle.'

People close to Laski felt that the loss of his libel action was a blow from which he never fully recovered. Outwardly he seemed to have changed little although, as time went on, he appeared to tire more easily but he steadfastly refused to take life more quietly. A colleague of Laski of those days commented to me that he 'simply could not stop accepting speaking engagements which became something of an obsession'.

During the General Election campaign of February 1950 Laski addressed upwards of forty meetings in thirty days and Norman MacKenzie has recalled to me that almost at the end of the run-up to polling day there was a Labour Party meeting at London's Conway Hall in Red Lion Square. 'Harold had already addressed a number of meetings that evening and I was at the door of the hall waiting to welcome him', MacKenzie told me, 'and when his car drew up and he stepped out I noticed at once how very ill he looked. I went forward to greet him and asked anxiously about his health. All that Laski said in reply, as he hurried into the crowded meeting, was "Don't worry about me. Look after yourself."' Laski was so obviously a sick man that the chairman thought of sending the audience home and later regretted he had not done so. However, although in evident distress Laski contrived to make a speech, which, the chairman said later, was eloquent and persuasive even if it lacked something of his usual fire.

Laski soon became really ill (an attack of influenza had been followed by a lung collapse) and his doctors decided that he should be transferred to St Mary's Hospital, Paddington. There, with his wife and daughter at his bedside, Laski died on 24 March at the age of fifty-six. He was writing to the end. On the very day of his death, a *Reynolds News* journalist received a letter from Laski (written only three days before) commenting on some observations the columnist had made about the rights of the King in refusing a Dissolution of Parliament and correcting what he considered to be a misunderstanding of the position.

And just before Laski died the *Daily Herald* published his last newspaper article. It appeared at a time of Fascist troubles in London's East End during which the Communists sought Jewish support. It was a subject on which he felt strongly, and in the course of the article he wrote:

> I know few realms of political behaviour where the Communist tactics have been more dishonest and more irresponsible than this. They ask for support from Jews on the ground that they, the Communists, are the only people who really mean to give the Jews safety, to suppress Fascism in all its forms, and to punish anti-Semitism with the severity its foulness warrants. They can promise everything to the Jews because they have no prospect in a foreseeable future in this country of having to make good the pledges they offer or to prove their wild charges against the Government in a court of law. But they say nothing about the harsh treatment of Jews in recent years in Russia and the countries under its domination.
>
> They are silent about Communist hostility to Zionism as a faith and of Communist punishment of Jews who seek to emigrate to Palestine. There is silence about the skilful exclusion of Jews from leading political positions, silence about the stern discouragement of Yiddish, with its remarkable literature and drama, and silent about the failure of the Russian attempts to make a Jewish national community within its own frontiers. In seeking to subordinate all thinking to the Party line there has grown up an ugly type of anti-Semitism in the area of Soviet influence which is intended to discourage, and, where possible, to destroy the Jewish hunger for fulfilment as a Jew.
>
> It is a change from the older policy of self-determination; and it is applied with the ruthless speed characteristic of the Communist

in power. He is friendly to Jews in Britain because he has used that friendship as a stick with which to beat the Socialist Government. He is unfriendly to Jews in the Soviet area unless they submit to whatever line of policy Moscow decides shall be imposed upon them. With the emergence of 'cosmopolitanism' as a deviation, the Jews, whose eyes are cast with longing on Palestine, are already in a zone of danger. That is the burden of every report which comes out of the half-hidden world where Moscow stands on guard.

Many tributes were paid in the national and international Press by leaders of academic and political life. Attlee, the Prime Minister, speaking from Chequers, said: 'He was a personal friend of many years standing and a man of outstanding gifts who had done great work for the Labour and Socialist movement. His brilliant intellect illuminated many of the social and political problems of our time.' The Director of the London School of Economics, Sir Alexander Carr-Saunders, said: 'The outstanding characteristic of Harold Laski was his generosity. He never spared his time, his energy or his money in his effort to help those in any form of need or distress. There must be thousands of people, and especially young people, who are in personal debt to him. He was no abstract theorist; he saw everything in terms of human beings and their wants. His was a life of devotion and sacrifice.'

There is a prophetic note in a letter, which is before me as I write, from Laski to a pupil of his who was taking a long time to make up his mind as to what he should write about. The letter, written in February 1950 reads: 'If you want to see me it really must be on the basis that you have made up your mind about what you want to do and how you propose to do it. I cannot spend a good deal of time watching you gaze at the stars without ever casting your eyes to the ground. In searching for some period the researcher has to decide on a subject. You seem to take the view that you have geological time at your disposal. I am in the miserable position of not belonging to this category.' When he wrote that, Laski had less than a month to live.

A former student of Laski recalled for me one of his teacher's last days at the School. 'He talked to me', he told me, 'as we were using the lift together, saying: "I have just concluded writing the obituary of the Lord Chief Justice of England for one of the national newspapers. I hope that, when it comes in due time to be published, it will be found that I have done ample justice to his great services to the State."'' Three weeks later Laski was dead whilst Raynor Goddard, then well over seventy, lived for another twenty years, dying at the age of ninety-four, in May 1971. Although bitter at the time about the way Lord Goddard had conducted his libel action, Laski bore him no lasting grudge.

Ralph Miliband said, shortly after Laski's death:

> Exhausted he was in the last years. Yet he went on, day after day, term after term, in School and out, travelling, speaking, writing, teaching. He did it simply, without fuss, out of a profound sense of duty, because he felt responsible and committed, because he was generous, in that most exacting form of generosity, generosity of self, because he was a craftsman and he believed that whatever one did ought to be done as well as was within one's power. He was an astonishingly hard-working person and it was difficult to realise that the apparent ease and elegance of his lectures, the depth of his scholarship were not only gifts of the gods; they were also the results of an industry that knew no respite. I first knew how really ill he must be when in the last few months he told me that he was very tired, and the admission, coming from him, frightened me. And next day he was back, laughing, full of life, and we would wonder and hesitate to tell him that he must rest, and hope that it was not so bad.
>
> And finally there is one incident that I shall always remember. It was the day he died, and such is the irony of fate, it was also the day on which a new Association of Political Science, which he was to have addressed, convened at the School. The chairman read a letter Harold had written the day before, apologising for his absence. One sentence of that letter remains with me because it tells so much of him. 'I hope', he wrote, 'that the Association will strike out boldly.' It is fitting that this should have been his last message. For he had courage and he gave courage to others. He had inspiration and he inspired others. His life and his work were a challenge from which we, who remain, must not shrink.

Following Laski's death a special issue of the School's magazine, the *Clare Market Review* was published and many tributes were paid by young men and women who had been in day-to-day contact with him. A young lady who acted as chairman of a Labour League of Youth meeting which Laski addressed recalled that:

> Three days later he sent for me. Before I learned the extraordinary range of his activities his interest in me seemed quite unaccountable.

He said it would be a good thing for me to study at the School. I explained that I hadn't matriculated, had left school at fifteen, and had to earn my living. But Laski's help didn't stop at encouragement and advice. He told me precisely for which qualifying examination I must study, how to study for it and finally made all the financial arrangements for my first lectures at the School as an evening student. He ended with a strict admonition that I was to see him every fortnight. This I couldn't bring myself to do. He was one of the busiest people I have ever known, and I was learning the lesson that first being with students and books has to teach—humility and the sense of one's own insignificance. Plentifully imbued with the latter I didn't dare to bother him. It was nearly two years later that I took my courage in hand and went to his room. By this time I had qualified to begin a degree, and I very badly wanted his advice. On the day, and in fact for days before, I rehearsed my 'statement' to him. It went 'Professor Laski, you won't remember me but nearly two years ago you were kind enough...' I knocked at the door. He called 'come in'. I went in, took a very deep breath indeed and opened my mouth... 'Well, well, old lady', he said, 'and how are you? Where have you been all this time?' It was the last time I let him surprise me. After that I began to regain my significance.

As one would expect, a host of anecdotes were recalled at the time. One was of Laski addressing a meeting at which he was being heckled by young communists. The meeting was beginning to show a readiness to turn the hecklers out when Laski interposed: 'Let them be. After all, we're all really Marxists together; they in their way and I in his.' One day he asked one of his staff at the School: 'Tell me, is———having an unhappy love affair? She's just handed me an appalling essay. If it's a love affair I won't say anything but if it isn't I'll have to talk to her.' (It *was* a love affair.)

The news of Laski's death brought tributes from over a score of countries and nowhere on the continent was he mourned more deeply than in France. His friend Louis Levy—author of *France is a Democracy*—spoke of the warm generous hospitality he found in Laski's home when 'exiled' in Britain during the war, adding: 'May an old friend say that his kindness to my compatriots was inexhaustible.' Levy said that it would not be difficult to write a whole book about Laski and France for he was soaked in French culture and particularly in French political thought. He said 'in France, Laski was of all British socialists the one for whom we all felt the deepest personal affection. I cannot forget that the last but one of all the articles written by Leon Blum was about Laski, nor how, in a conversation I had with Blum a few hours before his death, he told me in a voice broken with emotion that, in his view, the death of Harold Laski was an irreparable loss, not only for British Socialism but for the whole international Socialist movement.' Blum only outlived him by five days.

Levy recalled that twice after the war Laski represented the Labour Party at a French Socialist Congress and the ovations he received then showed the affection that French socialists felt for him. He reminded students at the London School of Economics that Laski, who had written a great deal on French philosophers and thinkers, was one of the most ardent admirers of the country's eighteenth century and that the nineteenth century was no less familiar to him. He went on:

> His contacts with French thought took him into earlier centuries too. His long-projected work on the political thought of the French classics was one to which all his friends were looking forward. Beyond that, none who knew Laski's passion for tolerance—surely the dominant aspect of his life—could be surprised at his astonishing knowledge of the sixteenth-century wars of religion in France, and their literature. Of all the historians of Europe, it was perhaps he who had gone deepest into the work of the great seventeenth-century Protestant pastor Jurieux.
>
> Although he spoke French with a strong English accent, Laski had a deep knowledge of the language, with all its shades and subtleties. He was too interested in ideas to trouble much about form but he felt the spirit of the French language. He had little taste for French poetry but he loved the rotundity of phrase and precision of meaning of our great prose-writers, and he appreciated to the full Voltaire's mastery of the brevity that in him is the soul of wit. Indeed, Laski saw the literary qualities of those whose ideas he disliked; he was captivated by the music of Renan's prose and wrote a brilliant little essay for the tercentenary of Bossuet, whose rolling periods enchanted him.... He knew most of the great French thinkers of our time and had often lectured at the Sorbonne and other institutions of learning. His works were known to thousands of French students, and some, which like the *Grammar of Politics* have been translated into French, have had a lasting influence.

As might be expected, Laski was on terms of personal friendship with many continental statesmen and he followed their fortunes with the keenest interest and sometimes anxiety. Lionel Robbins (now Lord Robbins) a contemporary of Laski on the teaching staff at the London School of Economics, recalls a conversation with him in the spring of 1948 when news came of the Communist *coup d'état* in Czechoslovakia which led to the resignation of the socialist Eduard Benes from the Presidency of the republic there and the tragic death of Jan Masaryk. Lord Robbins told me that he commented to Laski: 'These are disquieting events, Harold' to which, with tears in his eyes, he replied: 'Lionel, don't let us talk about it. I cannot bear it.' Lord Robbins, who at that time was Professor of Economics at the School, told me: 'I feel sure that any admiration Laski might have had left for Communist Russia was destroyed that day. The scales had indeed fallen from his eyes.' It will be recalled that shortly afterwards Benes, who had sought the restoration of prosperity and the preservation of the integrity of his country on the basis of the principles of democracy and international co-operation, too, was dead.

Whilst critical of Laski's political outlook and style of writing —including a display of what he called 'footnote erudition'— Robbins had said that he had complete facility in the Socratic method of instruction by cross-examination, and, in political theory, was 'truly masterly'. He had said in his memoirs that he would continue to think of Laski's love of books, of his impulsive generosity and sympathy with the unfortunate, and perhaps above all 'of that quick apprehension and sense of fun that so often, when we were on committees together, even at times of considerable dissension, would cause our eyes to meet in mutual relish at the absurdity of some pompous colleague or some preposterous academic formality'.

When the news of Laski's death reached Asia and Africa many tributes were paid to his memory by former pupils. Professor Julius Lewin, of Witwatersrand University in Johannesburg (once a pupil of Laski's at the School), wrote in a South African newspaper article: 'His absence of personal ambition strengthened the moral force that always lay close to the surface of his arguments' and 'his influence radiated out in a circle that was world-wide'. Another tribute: 'It was as a teacher that he was a giant amongst men; it was as a teacher that we loved him' summed up the feelings of many who wanted to let it be known that they had lost a friend.

Family man

Laski's funeral was at Golders Green Crematorium, and the Prime Minister and Mrs Attlee, with members of the Cabinet and other Ministers, were amongst a large congregation which also included diplomats, academics and students, many of whom could not be accommodated in the chapel. The committal was preceded by the playing of Chopin's Funeral March. No words were spoken and after a few moments of meditation the gathering dispersed.

Under his will (he left £19,558) Laski bequeathed everything to his wife 'as an expression of my loving devotion'. He expressed the hope that she would give some of his books to the London School of Economics and Lady Margaret Hall, Oxford (where his daughter had been educated), and 'one or more books' to named friends 'as a testimony of friendship'.

On top of everything else, throughout his life, one of Laski's liveliest interests had been collecting rare books and pamphlets, and wherever he travelled, both at home and abroad, he never lost an opportunity to wander leisurely around bookshops and see what he could find. Of one such experience, typical of many, he told his friend Holmes:

> I went into town bookhunting and bought Heylen's *Tracts* (1681) a beautiful folio at 6s.; and Bancroft's *Dangerous Positions* an historical defence of Elizabethan statesmanship. Then as the eye roamed it fell upon a copy of the first edition of *The Execution of Justice in England* (1584) which was by Cecil, Lord Burghley. It's worth say £12 but was unmarked. With a bounding heart I took it to the man (Jewish blood will tell) between two 1s. volumes. I asked him the price, he looked at the others, commented on the clean binding of the Cecil, and asked me 5s. for it. If you ask me how I got out of the shop, I frankly don't know but I still feel a tingling sense of pride at the find. One other amusing discovery was a volume of tracts on local government which had belonged to Charles Dilke.

Some time later he wrote to Holmes:

> I had a great book expedition in the East End of London; a queer old place in the Minories. No order, no shelves, all books in heaps on tables. Put in your hand and pick out what you can get. So I did. Shaftesbury's *Characteristics* three volumes, first edition, 3s. Pithou's *Libertes de l'eglise gallacane* a real beauty in perfect condition (1594), 1s. Huxley's copy of Gladstone's *State and Church* with a footnote explaining that Mr G. was a humbug, from Huxley to

Leslie Stephen who annotates with characteristic moderation: 'Perhaps he was but there were moments when he did not know it.' Also I have bought a curiously interesting book (1790) by one Lenormant called *J. J. Rousseau Aristocrat* which seeks to prove that J.J.R. did not help democracy at all and is a protest against the deification of him by the Jacobins. And a complete set of Richard Price's pamphlets (he was a theologian and pamphleteer who defended the American and French revolutions) with contemporary answers to them. I had never even heard of the shop, and—of its kind—it is far better than anything else in London.

As may be imagined, with book-hunting covering so many years, Laski built up a really remarkable collection of rare volumes which was one of the joys of his life. Full of enthusiasm, he would talk at length to his friends about them, correspond with owners of bookshops and private collectors and was thrilled and indeed excited when something came his way that he had wanted but never expected to find. He had hoped, in later years, to use his collection of rare books and pamphlets as a basis for further and more leisurely writing but, alas, it was not to be. In addition, of course, over the years, Laski built up a large working library which, after his death, was bought for the London School of Economics by a group of American friends.

The annual conference of the Labour Party following Laski's death unanimously passed a resolution declaring: 'This conference remembers with gratitude and affection the outstanding service rendered to the Labour movement, the cause of international solidarity and human freedom by the late Harold Laski and instructs the national executive committee to establish a permanent memorial to his memory.' An appeal fund was accordingly launched 'for an adequate capital sum to make possible the establishment of a worthy memorial'. A few months later a Laski Society was formed with Krishna Menon as chairman and an executive committee with H. N. Brailsford as president, Norman MacKenzie, secretary, and Lord Chorley, treasurer. It was planned to raise funds to help individual students, to reprint out-of-print Laski publications, to establish a 'Laski Room' at the London School of Economics, and to increase the value of a Laski scholarship. In addition, two of Laski's colleagues at the School, William Robson, Professor of Public Administration, and Kingsley Smellie (who succeeded Laski as Professor of Political Science) organised a collection, and with the proceeds it was decided to buy a Greek sixth-century BC vase as a token of remembrance. Displayed in the Founders' Room, it bears the inscription: 'In memory of Harold Laski. Given by his colleagues at the School.'

There was a widely representative gathering at a Laski Memorial Meeting held later at Conway Hall in the Bloomsbury district of London. With Lord Chorley in the chair, speakers who had known Laski through his various activities paid personal tributes. Ralph Miliband, as a former student, spoke of his warmth and humanity saying that Laski was interested in students because they were young, because the future was theirs and because he felt that through them he could influence the world. A London bookseller spoke of Laski's abiding love of books and said there were fewer places where he would have been more 'at home' than in a bookshop. James Griffiths, Labour Member of Parliament, told of evenings Laski had spent with miners in South Wales villages and of their feeling that he was 'one of us'. An Indian diplomat said that Laski had given the people of India confidence in themselves. Kingsley Martin spoke of Laski's capacity for teaching and H. N. Brailsford said 'here was a man who asked nothing for himself and sought only to serve humanity'.

Reviewing Laski's career, the *Manchester Guardian* said in a leading article that:

he was not a Manchester man for nothing. There was in him a strain of impenitent dissent and an attachment to liberty for its own sake that belonged rather to the Manchester Liberalism of the nineteenth century, whose economic founders he assailed, than to the Marxism that he tried to reconcile with British socialism. The slightest breath of injustice, any infringement of academic freedom, any subversion of civil liberty, whether well or evilly intentioned, any denial of a man's freedom to express his honest thoughts on politics or religion would bring Laski into action.... No one went to greater lengths to find historical explanations for Soviet Russia's hideous perversions of human justice. He tried to console himself with the belief —increasingly difficult to sustain—that, given peace, freedom would reassert itself in Russia, and that the age of terror and rigid conformity was a transient one. But, though this led him into odd verbal gymnastics. Laski never surrendered any of his own faith to the saving value of human freedom. It was his special contribution to British Labour politics and the theme of his best and most enduring writings.

The article goes on to comment that the outer world knew Laski best as a politician, 'his least successful side'. Many commentators and indeed friends both at the time of his death and since have said it would have been much better had Laski not entered the field of day-to-day politics. Professor William Robson, whom I have already referred to, told me he thought it would have been better for his reputation and standing if he had remained an academic and steered clear of practical politics. However, as Kingsley Martin put it, 'scholarship was overwhelmed by the political urgencies of the day'. Laski found it difficult to combine the role of *eminence grise* with that of popular leader and many uncertainties have been expressed as to the soundness of his political judgement. Ten years after Laski died, Attlee, writing on 'Leadership in Politics' remarked 'indeed people who talk too much soon find themselves up against it. Harold Laski, for instance. A brilliant chap but he talked too much. A wonderful teacher. You must be able to talk to teach and we need all the teachers we can get but he had no political judgement'.

But although Laski was sometimes criticised by his friends as well as his political opponents the *Manchester Guardian* commented that

few men of his generation gave more unstinted and unrewarded help to his Party. Labour owes him more than it recognised. The very diffuseness of his political activity weakened his academic achievement. He would have made a surer mark had he concentrated more on the fields of scholarship—and they were wide—in which he was a master. Not many of his contemporaries had his immense range of learning or his quickness of assimilation.... But it would not have been Harold Laski if he had chosen not to wear himself out as teacher and helper of young people, as drudge in public causes, and as generous and unfailing friend.

Ten years before he died, in his contribution to the *I Believe* symposium, Laski wrote: 'I have lived near great events and known men and women intimately who have served great causes greatly. As I look back I would not ask for wealth or power. I would ask only for the supreme gift of friends. That I have had in good measure. It has given me a sense of fellowship that has given to life a happiness beyond the power of sorrow to destroy.' I am sure Harold Laski would have endorsed that view at the end.

INDEX

Aptheker, Herbert 76
Attlee, Clement (later Lord) 53, 55, 62, 66, 71–2, 120–39, 162

Bacon, Alice (later Lady) 136
Baldwin, Stanley (later Lord) 48, 54, 59, 63
Beales, H. L. 35, 132–3
Beaverbrook, Lord 51, 129, 130
Beloff, Max 118
Beveridge, Sir William 18, 20, 51, 52–3
Bevin, Ernest 67, 71, 99, 124, 126, 130, 134
Brown, George (later Lord) 67

Carr-Saunders, Sir Alexander 53–4, 162
Carlton, H. C. C. 141, 142, 153
Champion de Crespigny, H. V. 140, 152
Chorley, R. S. T. (later Lord) 49, 50, 53, 168, 169
Churchill, Winston (later Sir) 2–3, 51, 56, 70–1, 84, 120, 121, 124, 125–31, 139
Citrine, Walter (later Lord) 68
Cooper, Duff (later Lord Norwich) 49
Craig, Yvonne, 40
Cripps, Sir Stafford, 49, 55, 56, 58, 65
Crowe, P. R. 23

Dahlastron, Warren 27
Dalton, Hugh 39, 46, 53, 126
Day, J. Wentworth 141, 142, 145, 146
Deakin, Arthur 124
De La Warr, Lady 9
Derer, Vera (nee Lewisohn) 42–3

Earnshaw, Harry 135–6
Einstein, Albert 85
Emerson, Rupert 27–8

Feaver, George 118
Firuski, Maurice 22
Frankfurter, Felix 11–12, 19, 71, 77–8, 116

Galton, Sir Francis 4
Gandhi, Mahatma 94–5
Gay, Ken 22
Gilmour, Sir John 61
Goddard, Lord 144, 151–2, 153–5, 162–3
Gollancz, Victor 63–7
Griffiths, James 169

Haldane, Lord 20
Harrington, Lucille 13
Hastings, Sir Patrick 145, 147–53
Healey, Denis 135–6
Henderson, Arthur 46, 47, 51
Herbert, Jean 30–1
Hillman, Sidney 86–7, 114

Holmes, Justice 12–13, 116
Horrabin, James 94–5
Hutchinson, John 29–30, 159–60

Israel, Myer 14

James, Wing Commander 68–9

Kahn-Freund, Otto 38, 101
Keene, Katherine 75
Kennedy, John 82–4
Kennedy, Joseph (senior) 82–4
Kennedy, Joseph (junior) 82–4
Kennedy, Rose Fitzgerald 82–4

Lansbury, George 9, 120
Lanyi, George 40–2
Laski, Diana (Mrs Matthewson) daughter 12, 21, 157–8
Laski, Frida (nee Kerry) wife 5–6, 9, 10–12, 18–19, 21–2, 77, 91–4, 156–7, 167
Laski, Harold: family background and birth 1; education, 3–6, 9; meets future wife and marriage, 5–6; estranged from family, 5–6; rejected for military service, 10; teaches at McGill University, Montreal, 10–12; birth of daughter, 12; Harvard University appointment, 12–19; involved in Boston police strike, 15–18; decides to return to England, 18–19; joins L.S.E. teaching staff, 22; reconciled with family, 21–2; remembered by students and fellow-teachers, 22–42; appointed Professor of Political Science at L.S.E., 25; wartime in Cambridge, 33–9; Fulham Council alderman, 44–5; invited to stand for Parliament, 45–6; U.S.S.R. speech criticised, 48–51; joins Socialist League and encourages Unity campaign, 54–7; attacks Communists, 58–9; supports unemployed marchers, 60–3; Left Book Club activities, 63–7; member of Industrial Court, 67–8; urges wartime socialist planning, 70–2; visits to USA and views on American life, 74–90; friendship with Krishna Menon and links with India, 90–4; attitude towards Israel and Jews, 95–9; political theorist, 100–19; chairman of Labour Party, 120–39; tries to remove Attlee from leadership, 120–6; 1945 General Election campaign, 123–31; meets Stalin in USSR, 137–8; presides over 1946 Labour Party conference, 133–4; visits Italy, 134–6; libel action in High Court, 140–55; happy home life, 156–7; attacks Communists' attitude to Jews, 161–2; illness, death and tributes, 160–70.
Books referred to: Studies in the Problems of Sovereignty (1917), 14, 103; Authority and the Modern State (1919) 103; Foundations of Sovereignty (1921), 14, 103; A Grammar of Politics (1925) 100, 103, 106; Communism (1927), 107, 113; An Introduction to Politics (1931) 100; Democracy in Crisis (1933) 107, 111; The State in Theory and Practice (1935) 106, 107; Rise of European Liberalism (1936) 106; Parliamentary Government in England (1938) 107, 108; I Believe (1939) 108–9, 170; The American Presidency (1940) 88; Revolution by Consent (1941) 107; Reflections on the Revolution of Our Time (1943), 111, 112, 113; Faith, Reason and Civilisation (1944), 111, 113; Trade Unions and the New Society (1949) 86, 114; The American Democracy (1949) 88–9; The Dilemma of Our Times (1952) 117.
Laski, Naphtali and Esther (grandparents) 1

Index

Laski, Nathan and Sarah (parents) 1–3, 5, 10, 21
Laski, Neville (brother) 155
Left Book Club 63–7
Levy, H. P. 155
Levy, Louis 164–5
Lewin, Julius 110, 166
Lippincott, Benjamin 31–2
Littlejohn, Edward 28
Lothrop, Donald 157–8

Macmillan, Harold 130
MacDonald, Ramsay 45–7, 48, 121,
MacKenzie, Norman 35–8, 107, 160–1, 168
Martin, Kingsley 24, 118, 169, 170
Matthewson, Robin 157
Mavalankar, G. V. 93
Mavalankar, P. V. 93
Maxton, James 50
Mehta, Gavenvihari, L. 104–6
Menon, Krishna 90–4, 168
Miliband, Ralph 23–4, 34–5, 163, 169
Morris, Sir Harold 67–8
Morris, Yaakov 95–9
Morrison, Herbert (later Lord) 70, 121, 124–5, 126, 130, 136

Nash, Paul 27
Nathan, Otto 85–6
Newman, Sir George 61
Noel-Baker, Philip 120–1

Odell, Charles 78–9
Opie, J. 146, 152

Palmer, Norman 94
Parlby, C. E. 142, 152

Paton, John Lewis 3
Pearson, Karl 4
Phillips, Morgan 57, 68, 102, 136, 138, 139, 155

Reith, Sir John (later Lord) 59
Rezneck, Samuel 29
Robbins, Lionel (later Lord) 166
Robson, William 100, 168, 170
Roosevelt, Eleanor 75, 84
Roosevelt, Franklin 75, 82, 84, 85, 100
Rothermere, Lord 54
Russell, Bertrand 15, 18

Sankey, Lord 46, 94
Sevareid, Eric 159
Siegal, Shirley Adelson 28–9
Simon, Lord 144
Singh, Gurmukh Nihal 94
Slade, G. O. 144–7
Stalin, Marshal 137–8
Steel-Maitland, Sir Arthur 51–2
Steer, E. T. 32
Strachey, John 55, 63–7
Strout, Richard L. 14

Wallas, Graham 18, 20
Warner, Wellman 30, 32–3
Webb, Beatrice 20, 23
Webb, Sidney 18, 20, 53
Wheeler-Bennett, John 102
Whibley, Stuart 81
Wilkinson, Ellen 55, 63, 66, 72, 121
Winant, John 75
Wolf, George 38–9
Wootton, Graham 101
Wright, Quincy 160